Public Relations For Musicians

*Your DIY Guide To Getting
Featured By The Media*

Bob Bradley

Updated - 2.2021

An unexpected life of public relations

Well, here we are! I commend you for taking those first steps and diving into the world of public relations for artists. Although the principles found in music PR are transferable skill sets across different industries, the music and entertainment side of things can require a bit more finesse and patience. For those who happen to have a communications degree, you have a great head start, and for those that don't, believe me, this isn't too difficult to grasp and really it's about taking in the principles and putting in the work.

The funny thing is that I never set out to have a career in this trade, and actually fell into it after some chance circumstances. As many can relate with, sometimes life works in mysterious ways, and often we simply correct course when needed. Those who are curious about the world of PR probably have a general idea of how the machine works, but many can become like deer in headlights when thinking of where to start and how the heck to take steps that drive results.

For a good part of the early 2000s, I either spent time in mortgage, slinging coffee at Starbucks or sitting in a 15 passenger van touring what seemed to be every city and venue imaginable. I was fortunate enough to have been signed to a large record deal, and with that came the obligation of hitting the road and promoting the music on behalf of the label, management, PR and others who had invested their time and belief in the music. You learn a lot from being a professional musician, and thankfully for our band, a couple of us had marketing in our blood to help us get to where we were in our careers. When the touring journey stopped, there was an opportunity to put those skills to use and even help others do the same.

After a bit of soul searching, I busted down the doors of a music media company and record label that I admired. I ended up securing jobs at both companies and learned the ropes of how executives handle marketing for artists at the upper echelon of independent music. In essence, it was the master's degree of figuring out PR and marketing whereas the touring was my internship, and the real-life scenarios and understanding both artist and business sides is something I was fortunate to grasp. In the years that followed I helped build other companies in music and worked with hundreds of other artists and companies that saw the value in what I had to offer. To this day, it's a work in progress, and learning is an everyday requirement to stay relevant and exciting.

There's a bit of mystique and often general confusion when it comes to public relations (or PR, media relations or whatever name you may have heard it go by). Of the thousands of people in music I have met over the past two decades, almost everyone has their own idea and sense of understanding of how the PR subgenre of marketing works. Many musicians pay little attention to PR, where other artists presume this is "Wonka's Ticket" to break through to new levels of success. I give the latter due credit for acknowledging PR's importance and potential but always caution myself to understand that PR is balanced with other marketing, networking and business type efforts. This is truly a sum of the whole scenario.

So, to tell the story a bit more, it was 2007, and after many years of touring in a full-time metal/rock band and being signed to a large independent label (Victory Records), I found myself working at a record label called Fearless Records and was assigned the role simply titled 'New Media'. I had no clue what that actually meant but quickly figured out it was the growing (yet oddly named) role of securing press on the Internet. Print media was still supreme, and getting a review in the local newspaper or via national magazines like SPIN, Alternative Press or

Rolling Stone was the holy grail of coverage. The Internet had plenty of great websites reviewing albums, and unique music websites like Purevolume and Myspace provided havens for music discovery and curation.

Going back decades, the average music consumer had to rely on the suggestions of their friends and family, walking into record stores, watching MTV or reading magazines like NME, The Source, Rolling Stone and Billboard to learn about the latest music trends. As the Internet became more and more dominant (and preferred), the playing field widened and political barriers of music coverage came down, allowing more artists of varied success to receive much-desired media coverage. I distinctly remember the days of walking into record stores, just to find out about what records new artists were releasing.

Fast forward to today, it's safe to say most music listeners discover their new favorites in both new and familiar ways. We have Instagram, Facebook, TikTok, Youtube, Spotify playlists and much more in addition to our favorite magazines, blogs, newspapers and video platforms. Some artists still advertise on billboards, others pay for full-page ads in magazines or sponsor bold posts on Instagram. It's far from necessary to do so and have success, which is a glimmer of hope since most simply can't afford those routes. There are so many ways to market yourself as an artist, but the focus here is on earned media, which is having music shared and written about without paying for it. This is what PR in my world is all about, and this book will help you plan your own campaign if you so desire.

I must preface this, nothing beats hiring a professional and I'm in no way suggesting that artists should think otherwise. As you wouldn't hire a guitar player or producer who has been doing it for a week, if one is in the position to spend the money I always say hire and partner with those that can do it better than you. However, I have met too many artists who simply lack the budget and even those who are curious about a career in PR. This book is for you, and if anything this is to provide you with the insight on how the world of PR works in our tech-driven society. Enjoy!

1 - What is public relations?

Seriously, what is this "PR" thing that perhaps some of your friends, fellow artists or even your industry mentors have mentioned at one point or another? We've heard this before, "what your band seriously needs is some good PR", as if this is the ultimate bit of late-night wisdom dropped on you at that party. Even better, a fellow musician brags on social media about all the media features they've received about their latest song and you're left feeling a bit confused, left out and even a little jealous. In most instances, we nod our heads and think, yeah we can figure this PR thing out when we have some time, and move on to business as usual. The truth is, most artists and the general public have little to no idea how this world of PR operates, but in reality, it takes very little time to get a strong grasp of its concept.

Public Relations, which will be addressed in this book as "PR", is essentially the standing relationship or perception that the public currently has about you. In the context of this book, I will be talking about PR and both teaching and coaching you on ideating, building out, maintaining and getting really creative with your overall artist brand. PR as a job or the efforts put into maintaining your reputation with the media is technically called "Media Relations", but in this book, I'm going to stick with just calling it PR for just about everything.

PR as a career, which I've been working in professionally for over 12 years, is the deliberate act of purposely creating and maintaining news, ideas, stories and anything else that is hopefully of notoriety to the public. The vehicle of this news delivery varies, but most commonly in the music industry this work is done via a publicist, manager or from the artist directly. The varied ways of delivering this news has expanded greatly since the internet hit our computers and smartphones, paving the way to easily communicate what is going on in the music industry. These news pieces are usually shared via social media, magazines, blogs, newspapers, Youtube, radio and television. Although most of us in music find out about the latest, most hype-worthy news via social media, the original information usually comes from one of these other sources.

The art of maintaining a strong, favorable public image of your art is not something that comes without effort. Each and every day is a new opportunity to creatively "get the word out" and connect with the audience through strategic efforts. It requires having a plan, and being realistic about what time you have available and identifying what is worth talking about. The truth is most of what is seen about a notable artist on the internet or in print was communicated and secured via a publicist.

What is also true, is that artists can also handle their own PR work if they learn the basics of communication, relationship building and creating a workflow that is reasonable to maintain. There are key elements that are needed for creating momentum and building out a consistent PR strategy as an emerging artist.

Critical information - What is the most important piece of news you could share?

Communication - What mediums of communication will you use to update the media?

Validation - Do you currently have any coverage of your music to leverage?

Earning interest - Do you feel confident enough to convince the media to tell your story?

Public opinion - How does the general public perceive your brand?

Persuasion - How do you want to shape the opinion of your brand?

Messaging - Everything that goes out into the world shapes the perception of your music

Critical Information - Here's the fun part, if you've ever met an artist (which we all have), you know we love to think everything we put into the world is important and groundbreaking news. "I just hit the studio!" or "Hey guys check out these awesome new pics we took with this famous photographer". It's good to be excited, grateful and enthusiastic about everything going on while making music and playing shows. However, I urge all artists to be mindful and empathetic to how the outside world takes in mass information and how they will perceive it. It gets more complicated with how the media and the general public digests the information, but let's start at the source.

It's wise to start with a single piece of information, something that is unique and that others would appreciate. Music is a beautiful thing because it is an interpretive piece of art and people usually have emotional attachments to the music and the artists behind the track. Many artists start with a single, or a focus track that will soon be released to the general public. Usually, this is a good piece of information to approach the media with, as this is information the media is used to receiving and talking about almost daily. Knowing what to push out via social media is one art form, but what to communicate with the press about is something usually much different. There is a connection between social media and the press, but we'll dive into that later in this book.

Knowing what the media likes to talk about is a great way to understand what information you would like to put into the world. I urge anyone to study and read music-focused blogs, magazines and newspaper columns daily to put yourself in the shoes of the writers you will potentially be building relationships with. What topics are they covering each time you visit the site? A review, new release, scandal, breakup, huge tour? Of course, and as an emerging artist, you really have to get crafty with the details to attract attention. Perhaps just having a new single isn't enough, as the appeal is really in the details.

Communication - Do you like to hit the phones? Or perhaps you are a bit reserved and prefer to stay on email? I urge you to identify your best strengths as a communicator and embrace it to take the time to accept and grow that communication style that is uniquely yours. Don't compare one artist to another on how they secure and nurture relationships, as what works for them, likely won't always work for you.

Does a friend always go to industry events, talk up a storm and end up with that press coverage you have been looking for? Great! Ask them for some tips and advice, but keep in mind that's not the only route to successful relationships with the media and garnering coverage for your music. Some people even use Twitter and social media to build relationships, but be careful and mindful not to step outside boundaries as some media strongly discourage sorting business inquiries through social media channels. Persistence and giving it a shot is key, and knowing what to say while respecting space is something to be cognisant of. Regardless of personality type, it's simply best to magnify the preferred way of communication and use it with finesse, daily.

Validation - The best way to build momentum is by having someone in the press or of notable status validating your existence. There are millions of artists out there, but has someone famous or a well-respected writer already sung the praises of your music? If so, you have a head-start that most other artists would die to have. While some media love a good exclusive or enjoy being the first to talk

11

about the next great artist, it's even easier to have existing coverage to wave around and say "hey, she likes it so maybe you will too".

Just like most things in life, including food, movies, cars, shoes and cat memes, if your friend or someone famous likes it, we pay attention and wonder what we've been missing out on. For those of us with kids or little brothers/sisters, look at "Baby Shark", by far the most infectious, viral (and perhaps annoying) song of a generation. Someone you know online talked about it, a friend shared it on Facebook, James Corden paid homage to it on television, but somewhere it started with a single source re-posting it, suggesting others should check it out for XYZ reasons.

There are varying degrees of validation, and it's only partially up to the artist to dictate how they want to be perceived and validated by the media and others. Once listeners and the media get their hands on it, the music then takes on a life of its own and grows from there. Look at a band like Radiohead, which in the eyes of the media and its fans may look much different from how the band itself sees their own music. Regardless, it's important to get validation of your band's existence and let the opinions flow as they may.

Earning interest - We'll dig into the finer details of this later on, but being able to get a hold of the media is just one level of the battle here. It's how one communicates their brand, music and what the important news is that can win over those relationships and secure that coverage. It's easy to source emails and phone numbers, but then what is said next can be the dealbreaker. Most of us in the media receive over 100 emails per day, not including the calls, Tweets and unsolicited social channel invites begging for coverage.

It's about asking for permission, making a warm introduction, understanding their audience and pitching a brief, but informative introduction to your music and latest update. If a prospective client sends me a personal message and I know 100% for sure it was meant for me, no matter what, I will respond one way or another. We are all human and want to feel appreciated and have our time respected. Even more importantly, using a strategy for communication will help persuade those in the media to consider what it is you have to offer.

To win over the time and interest of the media takes investment in understanding the offer you are putting into the world and why it would be worth anyone's time. I can't stress enough that every musician thinks their music is the most important out there, but it is the approach and details behind the music that wins over the invaluable attention that media can provide. Many of these writers are musicians themselves, or obviously avid fans of music and speaking their language and appealing to their preferences can be the difference between "hey what's up!" and delete ----> trash.

Public Opinion - The art of public relations is just this, the overall public opinion of your music, brand and overall ethos that encompasses what it is your music means as a whole. Perhaps most of you reading this book haven't been exposed to the public or in the media, but that will change and evolve as you start to play shows, stream music, sell some vinyl and win over quality coverage in the press. For those with some experience, there is a general or even polarizing viewpoint about your brand, and that can be changed with the right media communication.

Persuasion - What is the goal with all this PR nonsense anyhow? Are you trying to convince indie fans you're the greatest guitarist out there? As a DJ, are you looking to keep a cryptic image but be known for the craziest live shows? Or maybe as a hip-hop artist you are trying to be known for creating a new style or sub-genre. There are ways to deliver messages that in-turn cause action from the potential listener, and peak just enough interest to gain attention.

The attention span of your everyday music fan is slimmer than ever before, and one has to persuade that listener to give you a chance. The rabbit hole goes deeper since we first have to find the audience to persuade, but don't sweat things too much as this is a process that goes one step at a time (and then repeats, over and over).

Messaging - Every bit of information about your music and brand that ultimately comes from the source (you) further shapes how others perceive you. From a specific tweet, to an interview quote in a magazine or blog, the culmination of everything the public can discover about you matters.

This isn't necessarily a book on branding, but know that everything that you do for your artist brand adds up (including media placements, social posts etc). It's critical to remember that before, during and after any sort of PR push that every bit of effort and messaging matters and contributes to the whole.

2 - How public relations helps your brand

So what is the big deal with this PR stuff anyway? I mean, even though many of us have a rough idea of how the game works, how does it actually help your music and overall brand? The difficult part to wrap our heads around with PR is that it's not an exact science. One writeup in a local blog is not the key to what we all obviously want here, and is just a small part of how everything comes together. Sure, a killer review in a great magazine is a nice badge of honor and validates what you're doing, but what's next? Also, the "how" in how that feature was secured will vary from artist to artist.

There's a reason PR is approached in specific ways and abides by a certain set of standards. There are obvious benefits to working PR for your brand effectively, and here are just a few of the benefits of sharpening your PR sword and leading the front lines.

Message communication - This is the main prerogative with any PR firm, freelance publicist or ambitious artist you are pushing. What is the message we're putting out here? It's gotta be specific, and don't worry, it's smart and very normal to put out multiple messages every year, month or even weekly. The message is typically delivered via a press release, and sent to editors, influencers and specific journalists with a pitch or some sort of message conveying what the news or message is.

Sometimes news is brief, and sometimes it contains more information than the average busy person can possibly digest in one sitting. Sometimes, it's very necessary to avoid leaving critical details out. With music, I have found that brevity and getting to the point is more of a service to an artist than the opposite. At the end of the day we want to be noticed, and with PR it's really no different. We want our existing and new media contacts to notice what we are pushing into the world. It's often best to take a step back from what you're about to email or call someone with, and ask yourself "how would I react if I received this and had about 100 other emails in my inbox as well".

So now, consider the mission is accomplished and you've figured out the right pitch, have started a few conversations and now the press is starting to flow in. You're scratching your head wondering how all these multiple different features will help your career in the short and long term. Here's the truth, some of your press will organically help without you lifting a finger, but most of the benefits are reaped by ongoing cultivation of your brand, networking and successes in other areas of your music business. Yes, I said it, music is a business as well as a creative outlet, especially if you are reading this book. It sure beats shuffling papers for a living, so let's fully understand the game!

Reputation growth - Although most feel music should be done for the sake of the music, it's a bit of a letdown if only your Mom, Dad and best friend know about the music you're making. With every bit of media coverage outside of awareness, social media, streaming sites and live performances, the perception of your music and brand is being shaped. Who doesn't want to be admired and receive feedback (hopefully positive) on the music they make? The beauty of garnering results from PR, is seeing your story and reputation come to life through the eyes and ears of professionals who write about this stuff for a living.

Professional leverage - I can't even count the number of times I have been asked "How do I get a manager, booking agent or record deal?". One thing is for sure, in today's music business, artist development from scratch is not a common occurrence and most professionals want to see an artist reach certain milestones before taking a risk on them. The success of your brand is flexible but also grows together, so it's important to focus on the important tiers like songwriting, performance, recording, streaming and creative marketing.

Media coverage is sort of the icing on the cake, which ultimately isn't the end all but most people don't like cake without the topping right? A music industry professional who sees you have been featured in a handful of credible publications or blogs is more likely to take what you do more seriously. It opens doors, that is for sure. If you have strong media attention, lots of streams, Youtube plays, an amazing album/demo and a killer live show, I can assure you that you'll have a much better shot at getting what you want. However, every artist is at a different point in their career, I completely understand that, and the beauty of media features is that it will help attract more of the other tiers I've mentioned.

Backlinks - For those privy to the SEO game online, backlinks are simply having a link on one website link to your preferred source (your website, Facebook, Spotify, iTunes etc). Not only does it help improve SEO ranking, but it allows viewers and fans to be directed to the information most important to you as an artist. If you're trying to promote a tour, a new single, a new hairstyle or just getting started as a band, it's always helpful to have links to your music on other websites and social media sites.

Live shows + touring - Whether you are playing the dive bar down the street or preparing for your first direct support slot at a House of Blues, leveraging and experiencing the power of the secured press is priceless. The media secured prior to the show via event calendars, event previews and hype pieces can help with attendance and early perception and excitement towards your music. If media attends the event, then the promise of post-show features with photos provides even more coverage potential and shareable content for your social media. This stuff adds up, and imagine if you're doing this with multiple tour dates on your schedule.

More press - Yes, getting X amount of press can typically lead to even more press. Sometimes it happens without an effort, and most often you use your existing press as a "hey, I'm credible" calling card when pitching moving forward. Not too long ago I had one of my clients featured on a major entertainment publication online, and no kidding, within a day or two 45 other features went live without any additional work on my part. While this type of organic press on a mass level happens with celebrities, I can assure you this person was not a Kardashian.

The usual strategy is to let your contacts know within a pitch that you have been featured in other notable sources such as X, Y and Z. Don't forget to hyperlink those sources just in case they actually want to check. Sometimes if this contact wants to feature you, they may refer to another feature you sent them to brush up on why you are important. The goal here is to let them know you are credible, and to make their lives as easy as possible if they have interest in you.

3 - How the internet changed the PR game

What seems like way back, long before we found most of our new music on Spotify playlists and various blogs, there was a very controlled avenue of music discovery that was available. That was, and still is to a smaller degree, via printed magazines, newspapers and even "zines" which at least in some genres of music are do it yourself (DIY) print magazines created for a smaller niche. The magazines and newspapers relied on writers with their ears to the ground, attending shows and dealing directly with local bands, record labels and publicists to learn about new music.

Since being an artist and finding success was to a varied degree a lot more difficult in decades past, it usually meant if you had coverage in a publication that meant you truly had something going on. Most articles that you would see usually came from an artist signed to a label, and often those labels have tight-knit relationships which involved advertising agreements which led to editorial "love" via reviews, interviews and other types of features. This is by no means saying things operated in a "payola" type manner, but more so the route to coverage was direct and controlled for the most part so advertising and covering the artist in the same issue was very normal.

Fast forward to the late 2000s, the ascent and fall of Myspace and launch of iTunes, Facebook, Amazon Music and Ultimately Spotify directly changed the preferred way listeners like to digest music. Where before it was heading to the mall, visiting a listening station and finding killer magazines, now it's as easy as grabbing your phone, checking Facebook and going to Billboard.com to see what the latest and greatest is. The medium has changed completely, minus going to a live show (which I must stress, you can never beat the real thing). Print publications are still extremely relevant, and if anything they are more coveted than ever, due to so few good ones being left.

This is also a testament to their quality of content, great editorial coverage and showing long term value with the readership that they hold. If you have a favorite magazine, I encourage you to show them your support by subscribing, buying copies at the store and learning more about the owners and in-house + freelance writers at the sources. You can also find these people, just like online sources, on social media and mastheads on their digital versions to locate their appropriate work-related contacts.

I'm sure there are many (I'm thinking the old man yelling at the cloud meme) that blame the Internet for ruining their favorite print magazine or causing lost jobs at local newspapers. While in many ways this is absolutely true, I am taking a step back and just seeing the big picture here. The Internet is here to stay folks, and the changes they bring directly/indirectly are a result of how people prefer to consume media. In turn, the creatives build those new platforms for music discovery.

Nothing beats a great editorial on an emerging artist, but now it just happens to be online and viewed over mobile, laptop, desktop computers and tablets. Although I haven't met many who read magazines on a tablet (yet), I'm sure there are enough to warrant their creation.

With more quality blogs and online zines at your fingertips via mobile, iPad and laptop, the ease of technology has opened the floodgates for incredible writers from around the world to write about artists large and small. You can be an artist from New York, but get coverage from blogs in Canada, Turkey, Germany and other countries with ease. Decades back it just wasn't that easy, and with the majority in print in the past, the lead times and requirements of physical products limited the opportunities. Now, it's possible for an emerging artist, perhaps you, to secure dozens of quality features in these sources worldwide.

With pitching over email instead of sending your CD - which is very expensive - to all these different sources and playing the waiting game, you never knew where you might end up weeks or months later. True, we still had the internet and email then, but the Gatekeepers, including labels and publicists, had a lot of control over what went into those publications. Independent artists had a much harder time before, but today it is so much easier. If anything, it can be overwhelming because there are so many great sources available to artists to submit their music to. My challenge to you is to curate these sources that have the most meaning to you and get to know their content.

4 - What is your story?

Okay, before you hit the ground running on launching your own PR campaign, it would be ideal to know why you're doing this in the first place. Obviously your music is amazing, well-written, expertly produced, mixed by a legend and now set up for distribution on all platforms. However, ask yourself why you are doing this music thing. This is a mindset game more than anything, I want you to dig into your purpose as an artist and think of yourself as a messenger of something bigger and potentially timeless.

I can't even count the times I've consulted with an artist, and I asked them "what's the story of you as an artist and what makes you different from the rest?". A lot of the time it's a deer in the headlights, and that's okay since I get paid to pull these things out of people. However, if you're going to go it alone, I strongly recommend sitting on the mountain and thinking about the big picture. It's also a good time to remind you that PR is under the wing of marketing, so to potentially attract millions of people out there to find your music, they need memorable impressions of your music and brand.

The beauty of the music industry is that every artist has a different background, upbringing, musical style, set of influences and so much more. Even though many artists may share similar sounds, when you dig deeper you get to know the artist as a whole, and that makes things even more interesting. Often for a major label and top-selling artists, fans look to websites and blogs to learn more about their history and upbringing, which in itself creates conversations that lead to more awareness of the artist. The great part of a unique story is that you can leverage that as an emerging artist to bring further interest in your growing music career.

So, how do you figure out what your story actually is? It's really not that hard, and I don't suggest driving yourself crazy trying to identify the details.

Self-Interview - Many publicists, ahead of any actual confirmed interviews from blogs or magazines will provide their client with a set of questions to be answered for informational and media press reasons. If you're handling your own press, I suggest asking a friend, fellow band member, producer or even family member to put together a set of questions about your music, career and background. You can always write your own questions as well, or simply search for artist interviews online and copy what questions are asked on there.

As you complete these answers you'll find that your story comes out, and along with that the core values of why you do what you do. The cool part is when you are done, you can even pitch this completed interview to a website for publishing. It's like a double-win with a single effort, and you'll develop a better sense of what your story is as an artist.

Video Media Kit - This type of content typically lives on Youtube, Vimeo or even Facebook, and is shot professionally and edited to be brief, informational and live as a sort of a profile on your artist brand. A warning to musicians, this approach can either come out as something inspiring and groundbreaking, or can end up looking desperate and tarnishing your marketing efforts. While I don't see many alternative lifestyle artists doing this (metal, punk etc), perhaps it may work better for professional session musicians, pop artists or even DJs looking to promote their business.

If there's any sort of doubt of making this type of clip public, simply make it private on Vimeo or Youtube and simply share with those who would appreciate the information. I encourage you to take a look at your genre of music, agenda with your work and to consider if this is a good fit for telling your story.

Artist Background - Are you a musician with a history of playing with other notable bands or even touring with other musicians? Your history and association is a stamp of approval for critics who may have never heard of your current work, but perhaps may know of some of the artists you have associated with in the past. Think of it this way, in business or even at parties, one of the first things people discuss are friends or professionals they have in common., It's a way to create common ground and eases the conversation to grow in progressive directions. You may also be asked about where you have worked before, and this is all in an effort to find similar ground.

Music relationships with the media work the same way, especially if this isn't your first rodeo. Often artists don't make the effort to flaunt their resume, which may miss you opportunities to fast forward to securing quick press and relationships that can help you over time. This is especially true if that person is familiar with your past work or associated musicians, producers etc. As an example, if an unknown artist sent me their music with zero background I may just not take the time to give it a listen. On the other hand, if that same artist mentioned a member or two were in former bands I loved, and/or they had their music mixed by someone who I appreciate, I just may give it a spin.

This is all part of your story, it's the who, what, when and where that you tie in with anything fresh about your band, including the music, artwork, track listing and press photos. One other thing I must add is when putting this information together for the media, do not forget to keep this short and sweet. Later on in this book, I'll give you an example press release for you to use for inspiration. This is how I learned how to write press releases and to pitch, I analyzed the work of my mentors and found examples on the Internet. Find what works, and make it your own.

5 - Where to start

There are so many thoughts, ideas, to-dos and maybe doubts running through your mind right now. I have all this great music, ready to release, but the idea of doing this PR thing on my own seems overwhelming. I understand it seems like a lot and even though there have been some great ideas and even steps discussed in prior chapters, it's still important to have a game plan that is simple and well laid out. To start off a great PR campaign requires some prep work that may not be easy for all projects and artists, as it really depends on what you are creating and pushing.

This book was written throughout late 2019 and early 2020, so what the marketplace demands at the time of publishing may be different if you're reading this a few years down the line. What hasn't changed though is having a good strategy for releasing your music and ultimately pushing it to the media. People can only take in so much information at once, so it's good to have what it is that you're pushing prior to putting things out into the world.

Perhaps you have a full-length album, a couple of music videos and some decent press photos ready to go. Oh great and that's exciting news! I have a list for you below of things that I recommend you prepare before you release your next single, EP, album or music video. One thing to note is to focus on quality over quantity. If you don't have a high standard for the content you already have, it may be good to get a second set of eyes on your project or additional advice from music industry professionals to help get dialed in. For example, you may have 10 great songs mastered and ready to go, but the artwork is less than appealing and the press photos are not of high quality, that may hurt your chances of getting the attention that you deserve from the media and ultimately potential fans.

This is where a lot of artists make a huge mistake. They spend so much money making the music or video, but then they forget to save money or be considerate about their marketing budget. In the context of this book, I'll refer to the marketing budget as assets used to promote yourself in addition to anything spent on social media advertising and even print. This is also relevant because the media are the gatekeepers they can get more eyeballs on your brand. So it's good to be mindful of what your marketing assets are. Don't worry though, I know from experience that there are ways to make all of this work even if you don't have much of a budget or even anything at all to spend.

Photography - One of the first things that people see when they read an article about an artist is the photo of the group or artist. We typically refer to this as the press photo, and you can have one or preferably at least a few available to hand off to media contacts. To get specific, have at least one photo that is horizontal in formatting as that is typically the standard that most websites, magazines and newspapers use.

Be mindful of having high-quality photos available, not only photos but ones that truly represent you as an artist and that make a great impression. Whether they are offbeat and artistic in style, or straightforward as you would see from any major or independent artist, really think about how you want to be perceived. Thankfully, it's pretty rare to see an artist miss the mark on photos in the Press, but then again I think that half the reason they are being featured is that they have great photos to begin with.

There's nothing wrong with taking your own photos or asking a friend using an iPhone to snap some photos to start with. I would recommend using post-photography software such as Photoshop or free programs online to touch up and give your photos a little bit of life. If you can afford it, find a photographer in your network or do some research to find a good fit that represents your style and meets your budget. I would lump this marketing expense into the highest priority slot.

Artwork - Having great artwork years ago was probably a higher priority on my checklist then it is today. I think artists typically know what they want in art and that tends to take care of itself, but once in a while I see artists try and handle their own artwork and it just doesn't look great. This is where I once again ask you to get second and third opinions from trusted peers and even a music industry professional on the artwork that you currently have. If you don't have artwork yet, and you can spare the expense, hire a professional.

90% of the time listeners are going to see your artwork as a small square on Spotify, Apple music or on YouTube and it just doesn't have the same effect as it used to have when CD sales dictated much of an artist's income and success. Regardless of when it comes to working with the media and pushing your release to them, having your artwork in your asset folder ready to send to the people upon request is important. If you have fantastic artwork that is eye-catching and even better, tells a story, that is just icing on the cake.

Promotional Copy / Bio - This part is a little tricky, because in my opinion most long-winded artist biographies tend to be too self-indulgent and not worth reading. Perhaps years ago that was a different story. But now with time being even more valuable than ever, it's important to be mindful of brevity when describing yourself as an artist. This promotional copy that you should develop can be anything from one paragraph to multiple, depending on how much you want to speak of regarding your career and brand.

The purpose of this promo copy, or bio is to give the media a brief bit of background on who you are as an artist, where you come from and what it is that makes you amazing. I won't put any full example biographies in this book, but I do suggest hopping on Facebook or Google to look up bios from some of your favorite artists. Note some of these will be a lot longer than you will ever need for the time being, but it'll give you a good idea of what I'm talking about.

This bio can be used across the board with your social channels as well as your press efforts. And for the purpose of this book and for the efforts of PR, I always provide this with all of my press releases and pitching so the media can have an easier time writing features and reviews about my clients. I stress again, keep these paragraphs to a minimum.

Additional promo materials - Besides the aforementioned bits of information that are the bare minimum for effective media pitching, it's also good to take some time to think about other things that could be useful. One obvious list would be any previous press that you may have secured before launching into this new or first time media campaign. Have you been featured in any notable blogs, magazines or newspapers before? Awesome, be sure to mention that since that gives you potential credibility.

Other items to consider would include music videos past tour or show information and really anything interesting that would make you stand out. Are you an accomplished artist and happened to do your own artwork, be sure to mention that! Were you in any prior bands that had success or have current members in other groups more successful than your current project? Be sure to include that information as well. This is really about collecting and making available a minimum, but effective arsenal of information and assets to ensure your best shot at the media taking a feature to the finish line.

6 - Why relationships matter

Although the sum of this chapter may come off as a topic that is obvious and a no-brainer for most of us, it still needs to still be addressed in the context of PR and your overall marketing based mindset. A relationship with the media is different in music than it may seem in other industries, and this is not the same type of dynamic that would exist with a manager, a booking agent or even a record label. Your relationship with the media is everything, especially when you are not at the level of a Snoop Dogg, Metallica or any multi-platinum artist that most likely will garner press without much effort upon announcing new music or any large worldwide tour.

As humans, we tend to be attracted to and admire other people that understand and resonate with us. A great relationship with the media is a genuine effort made with a "one by one" mentality. Yes, there are thousands of great writers and people of influence in music but you can't get to know them all at once and indeed, it takes a lot of patience. It doesn't mean that you shouldn't think big and try your best to build out a quality list of contacts. This is just a reminder that the journey taken with great relationship building is actually a career-long effort and something that happens day by day.

Remembering back to the late 2000s when I started working in PR for the labels, I was fortunate to have a built-in system (AKA the brand power of the label) to get me in the door with many of these people. Many of these contacts I was simply introduced to, but after that moment the quality of the relationship was 100% up to me to maintain moving forward. The truth is that everyone is going to have both advantages and hurdles when giving the PR thing a go. Although I was thankful for the backing of a great label and mentor, I really had zero idea how to do the job and had to ask plenty of questions, do my research and allow time to build up experience. The goal of this book is to fast forward past some of the clueless parts and use your transferable skill sets to crush it at the PR game.

Keep in mind, those who work in the media and cover music/entertainment are tasked with sometimes challenging assignments when covering that album, single, live show or even interviewing people in-person or over the phone. There are a lot of hoops to jump through to get from A to Z, and their perception of the people (you) they are working with throughout the process is very influential to the outcome. This is, of course, only applicable once a magazine, newspaper or blogger has even responded and then has agreed to cover your music. Typically, in a label arrangement, the PR person who is in-house or hired as a consultant is positioned to reach out to the media to secure these on behalf of the artist. For you, this will likely be a situation where you reach out directly, acting as both artist and PR.

If you don't have any media relationships yet, I recommend once more referring to the prior chapter "Where to Start" and being mindful when gearing up to handle your own press. Without knowing how to start the race, and how to run in what shoes, you'll end up falling down rather quickly and spoiling most of the efforts you put into your PR work. Before you send that email, make that phone call or send an email blast, put yourself in the shoes of the busiest person you can imagine. Just as you would in a professional work situation, or with a friend/family member you respect, be yourself but also know every interaction with the person is a direct reflection of who you are and how you will be perceived.

7 - The art of the follow-up

When pitching the media on any level I can't stress enough that a good amount of your results will come down to one thing...the follow-up. Yes, it's so simple it's almost scary. You send that amazing pitch out about your music, days or weeks go by and ugh, nothing at all. Don't hang your head down in defeat, as 99.9% of the time, it's nothing personal unless there's something I don't know about here (only kidding). I present this chapter with caution though, since we will remember that we're dealing with people here and everyone is different and has different communication preferences.

The follow-up is something that more often than not, gains closure on the effectiveness of the pitch. The usual scenario is that your pitch was either reviewed and passed, saved for later, deleted immediately (remember, nothing personal) or someone simply just missed it. Some of these writers, reporters, editors and other gatekeepers receive dozens or even hundreds of pitches every single day. Even the most seasoned and respected PR professionals see many if not most of their pitches go without a response for the simple reason that they are busy and can only pick and choose what best fits their immediate needs. The point of all of this is to follow-up in a way that avoids coming off as spammy, repetitive or harassing. The goal here is to avoid being a toddler tugging at our jeans asking for ice cream and doing it in a way that hopefully gets what you want.

I would say the best amount of time to give before a follow-up really depends on the timeframe of your campaign and impact of a release, tour or major event. If you have an album coming out and your pitch went out at least a month before, great, that gives you some breathing room and sets you up to follow-up a week or two before release. This also lets some time pass before the follow-up, allowing your contacts to potentially have that needed time to go through their cue of pitches, check out your music and set up that feature. Responses could possibly include just what you were hoping for, like "hey Sarah, yeah we got your pitch and we're actually including it in our roundup of reviews coming up in the next week or so". Or it could be "Hey Jim, yeah I saw that but unfortunately, we're gonna pass for now.". Or, even better, to prove the point here, you may see a response like "I didn't see this, thanks for sending and yeah I'll check it out".

In the case they didn't see your pitch the first time, I give you permission to follow-up one more time after another week (or ideally two) at the earliest. This is where taking impeccable notes is critical, since you've gone down the rabbit hole of pitching a wide variety of contacts to your latest music, but now it's happening in different intervals for different people. This is where I recommend self-reporting, so you know who you are having conversations with and at what day/time. Using sources like Google Docs, Microsoft Excel or free/paid project management software is an excellent way to keep track of everything. Preferred sources vary by person, but usually, if you're doing things yourself (DIY) I recommend starting with an Excel or similar platform and evolving from there.

The point of keeping track of your pitches and conversations is to have self-accountability and to have a point of reference when following-up and with whom. I leave this up to you when you make the follow-up, as it's really a matter of the timeline of your release, and when you start pitching. I can't stress enough though, do not follow-up the next day or preferably within days unless there is a conversation in process and some sort of commitment made. That being said, since we're about halfway through the book...here's what a timeline may look like for following-up when pitching your own music.

The pitch - Now that you understand how all the pieces come together and how results are secured, where do you start? Most importantly, when you have everything put together for your next album, single, show, tour etc it's time to really dig deep and figure out WHY you and this music stands out from the pack. It's said that over a million releases come out per year thanks to the ease of music creation and distribution, so at the end of the day there needs to be that "angle" that makes you different. Sometimes it's simply the music, and while that's most important, we all know that many famous artists are worth talking about for so many other reasons.

So when you're crafting that email or preparing to hit the phones, think about what it is that makes the music special and if anything about your story or brand can pique interest. I highly suggest taking notes along the way, especially if you're still in the process of creating your next piece of work. If you're in a band or working with others, begin a conversation about this to see what awesome ideas you can pull together.

Individual conversations - You have a few responses or callbacks. AWESOME, you're doing something right and it's important to take note of what those steps were that you took. Remember the script you used on the phone, save a draft of that email, and remember what's working as it's often difficult to break through to these gatekeepers. It's a no-brainer philosophy, but take what works and keep doing that..and for what doesn't...do something different.

While you don't want to sound like a robot when calling or emailing the media, it's also good to at least sound like you know the lingo and how to sell yourself. Making a good phone call with a voicemail is always helpful, especially in today's society where most prefer email and texting over any in-person or phone interaction. This approach can make you more memorable, or at least increase the chance of getting a response as you pitch throughout the months (or years).

The follow-up - If you have an initial response from a media source, or even an ongoing conversation about your release in play, it's important to know when and when not to follow-up with these sources. This is where I stress keeping an excel type document with reporting on any active conversations about your release. In this document you can notate what your last conversation was about, and if they committed to anything specific or even mentioned when you should reach back out. For the most part, these people keep notes as well so they keep track of the million other projects they have going. So you should do the same, as it will keep everyone sane.

As the release date approaches for your music, or at least enough time has passed since your original pitch (say a week or two, it all varies) it's good to revisit your list to check the status of all your conversations. This allows you to go down the list one by one, following-up accordingly with each source in the way that best respects the relationship and timing of press commitments. So if someone responds with "that's great, I'll check it out", don't follow- up the next day, but maybe the next week or closer to the actual release date of the music. For someone who commits to something, just be mindful of any requests they have, or of any assets you can send their way to make the process as easy as possible. Every conversation can be different, so it's good to treat it individually for those obvious reasons.

For those that never responded to your initial pitch, I stress that a follow-up blast is always an equal risk of annoyance and securing interest in your music. For one, DO NOT send off a BCC email or newsletter blast of the same exact pitch to your list a second time. That runs the chance of unsubscribing or getting chewed out from select contacts who maybe saw it the first time and were not interested.

The best approach is to come up with something fresh to come back to your list with, perhaps a music video or tour announcement in support of the music you originally pitched. This way if someone missed your first pitch, it doesn't come off like you're nagging them with the universally dreaded (did you see my email pitch?) type approach.

Release date pitch - So the day comes, the new album, single or music video is finally live and you're excited to tell the world. It's a huge day, and many of us know how thrilling it is to know our creative works are out in the world. While every approach to pitching and follow-up is different, I've found if you already pitched the news prior, it's not always good to send the "out now" pitch again on release day. If anything, it may come off like spam, especially if you put it in a newsletter format.

However, if you are looking to pitch this new release for the first time (nothing prior) or even after release, typically this is fine to pitch on a mass or individual scale to the media. This is why follow-ups on an individual level are always best, especially since you can address the specific conversations you may have been having along the way.

Additional follow-ups - Sometimes we all get so busy, that things completely fall through the cracks. I give you permission to follow-up consistently. But there are those that are committed to coverage of your music but haven't followed through with said feature. If anything, they may appreciate the occasional reminder and you win since sometimes it's easy to walk away if things fail to come to fruition after a promised media feature. Be persistent about it, but play nice, be thankful and keep the follow-ups spread out by multiple days or even week(s) to avoid being a pestering musician.

I can immediately think of many times when media person X promised me a feature, but then fell off the face of the earth for a week or two. After a couple of follow-ups they responded with something like "OMG I'm so sorry, XYZ happened but now I'm back and I'm ready to post your feature". People often appreciate the reminders, and by staying on top of it in a nice way, we can assure these promised media features see the light of day.

Here are some quick rules of pitching and follow-ups to post on your wall:

DO be respectful in all email and phone communication about your music pitch

DO be as individual as possible with outreach and follow-up on your pitching

DO show gratitude when someone in the media features your music

DO keep your pitching and follow-ups short and sweet

DO include critical information and asset links in all communications

DO NOT be rude, emotional or spiteful if someone rejects your music or provides feedback

DO NOT email, call or blast duplicate pitches to the same contacts throughout a PR campaign

DO NOT forget to keep track of your conversations, you want to remember all the details

You get the idea, just be mindful of these things for each and every email.

8 - How to measure PR results

As a publicity professional playing the PR game for well over a decade, one of the most frequent questions I get from music clients is "how can I measure these results?".

Especially as industry and marketing strategies evolve, and we now live in a marketing world focused on Key Performance Indicators (KPI) or what may just be called metrics. Specific numbers are a great way to show how the results actually affect your overall growth in awareness and potential sales outcome.

Here's the truth with music and media, it's very hard to pinpoint where your exact successes are coming from. Outside of Oprah putting your vinyl underneath each guest's seat, or having your song on the biggest playlist or television shows out there, it takes a little combination of logic and figuring out specific numbers to best calculate your results. Remember that we are talking about websites, magazines, newspapers and social media channels, and they all have specific overall followings which then have to be narrowed down to a potential amount of eyeballs and ultimately action taken.

Not only does the reader have to actually engage with your press feature, but they also have to take action by visiting your profile on Spotify, buying merchandise off your website, going to a show or by sharing that feature on their social media. While many artists simply want to be featured in the media for the prize of being acknowledged by their favorite website and their following, others use this as a tool to build a following, streams and sales numbers with merchandise, live shows and physical music products.

Website and Magazine Following - So you have finally scored a great feature in a notable magazine or on a popular music website. Now you're wondering, what does that mean for my success? I completely understand you sunk money into making the music, mixing, mastering, art and more. Now you're wondering if the juice is worth the squeeze with this media stuff. It feels great to have the feature, and now you sit back, waiting for some sort of measurable result. You get a text from a friend, "Hey Sarah, saw you on Pitchfork, great feature and congrats!".

Although I won't expect many of my musician readers to dig in obsessively on this topic, however, if you're interested in publicity as a skillset or as a potential career, I would recommend providing some sort of statistics to your music client. Each magazine has a "media kit" and "editorial calendar" which is available upon request or sometimes hosted on their website (about section, advertising etc). A print magazine media kit should disclose distribution numbers for the magazine, in which countries, and potentially how many issues have been put out there into the world. From that point, there's no guarantee on how many eyeballs you'll get on the feature, but those numbers are good for disclosing "potential max impressions" on your name.

Now if you're on the cover of Billboard, that's pretty much a sure shot that every reader of the magazine is going to get an impression of your name. However, if you have a small quarter page review or just your name mentioned a few times in an article (which is still great!), you will obviously understand your name will not reach every reader. It's good to understand this, to best manage your expectations and to keep track of these things for each feature secured.

For websites, it's a lot easier to measure with a few things in mind. Every website, even by subpage, can be measured for total visits, pages visited, average duration on the website and even the bounce rate. This is a great way to vet websites as well, especially if you are considering the advertising side of things. You may be told by people that X website gets 100,000 views a month, but after visiting a site like Alexa can find the truth that they only get 1,000 per month. Or quite the opposite, where you think Y website is "cheesy" but you check the metrics and realize they are a top visited blog.

For the sake of keeping this book relevant, I'll just mention the most popular website for measuring web traffic is Alexa (not the Amazon speaker) and there are alternative sources online that are both free and paid. The goal here is to be discerning with who you spend your time pitching and securing media with, but also while keeping an open mind as a great PR campaign is sometimes the sum of the whole.

Especially from a web traffic, search standpoint, having dozens of great features on your band can lead to organic reach, especially knowing each online feature should have links to your website, web store or streaming sources for your music. All of these elements add up to better online discovery, but I'll save the finer details for the search engine optimization (SEO) experts out there.

Streaming Numbers - Although the topic of music streaming is quite polarizing, one thing we can all agree on is that discovering and finding great music is now easier than ever thanks to Spotify, Apple Music, Amazon Music, Youtube Music and the plethora of other competitors out there. While playlisting is another great form of PR exposure, what I'm speaking of here is measuring an uptick of plays after a larger media feature goes live on your music.

For example, a large magazine or website feature goes live regarding your music. Be sure to ask the source to embed a music player from your preferred streaming destination like Spotify, Youtube, Apple Music, Bandcamp or whatever source is relevant at the time of reading this book. This will allow readers to listen to the music natively on their website without leaving to visit a different destination. Keeping everything, including your music being promoted native to this specific website allows the listener to fully immerse themselves in your music brand while increasing your streaming stats at the same time.

In general, if you are starting to rack up great media coverage, there's a good chance your streaming numbers will increase organically as well, due to the curiosity from listeners eager to learn more about your music and brand. It's important to keep track of these changes in numbers, at least on Youtube, Apple Music and Spotify. There are also backend tools within many of these platforms that can provide in-depth metrics and pinpoint where the streams are coming from. For example, with Spotify, visit Artists.Spotify.com and for Apple Music visit Artists.Apple.com to sign up and keep track of your impressive growth around the world.

At the end of the day, in addition to the feel-good notoriety of getting your music heard and praised, it's super important to get those streaming numbers up and if you find that certain types of press, in certain regions of the world, yield higher numbers and responses be sure to add more fuel to that fire. The point of this whole PR process, while always learning along the way, is to find out what works and pull back on what doesn't serve you.

Social Media Engagement - As you begin to secure more press in the media you may notice an increase in likes, followers and comments on top social platforms like Facebook, Instagram and Twitter. If you post video content on IGTV, Instagram Stories, Snapchat or Tik-Tok, be sure to keep an eye on increased engagement via those platforms as well. A trick with all this press is to ensure you share this via social media as a link to the feature or by creatively making videos promoting it. We're looking for any excuse to post something awesome on social media, as selfies get old and nobody wants to see your album cover every single day. So post your great media coverage, and note the source that featured you will appreciate it as well if you tag them.

If a certain feature goes live, make sure they share the feature on their given social media territory as well. There's a good chance you will receive new followers, likes and comments from that. This once again gives me a chance to remind you that this is all the sum of the efforts, and the general rule of thumb is that potential fans may not check out your music until they have seen your name close to 10 times overall. So if they see you in a magazine, on a website, shared all over Facebook feeds and randomly on Instagram or Tik Tok videos, maybe they will *finally* be curious enough to give you a shot.

Increased Sales - Here's an exciting one, if sales numbers begin to pick up as your PR efforts make progress, you're surely doing something right and reaping the rewards quickly. While I would personally consider streaming numbers and the money earned from that as sales, I am referring more to things like sales of merchandise like vinyl, t-shirts, CDs and even MP3s from online stores like Bandcamp. Selling one t-shirt is the equivalent of thousands of streams of one song, so it's important to remember to push links to your website or store when securing features with the press. While a link to your site/ store may happen organically if you provide this information upfront, it's also important to ask the writer if they can include any preferred links.

Think about it this way, you have a new single or album coming out, and you have CDs, vinyl, cassettes and new shirts being made, you surely want to promote that. I've seen thousands of news pieces on new artist releases, and while it may have a link or embed to their music there is usually a lack of outbound links to sources to pre-order or purchase merchandise. What if I'm head over heels in love with a new song I hear, but am just lazy enough to avoid buying something if I don't have a call to action (link etc)? But if there is a link and information about "limited vinyl available for pre-sale" included for only $15 and I'm feeling euphoric about what I just heard, I may just click on that and score you another sale.

Sales for artists is about support, emotional decisions, excitement, convenience and timing. All these things need to be kept in mind when promoting your music and making things available for the media. Ultimately, you are creating a brand that is tied to your music that is hopefully "sharable" for so many exciting and compelling reasons. The media is here to help amplify the efforts of artists, and getting those sales and royalties is a great way to keep reinvesting in yourself and future PR/Marketing efforts.

9 - How to write a press release for music

As with so many industries, there are universally recognized forms of communication and ways that individuals and collaborators in any given field "speak". While it may be tempting to reach out to specific publications about your music without additional information, strategy and background, this may decrease the chance of getting coverage for many reasons. So, in addition to providing sources in the media with links to your music, press photos and obvious basic information relevant to the music in question, there is a critical and widely utilized piece of information most likely to receive. You guessed it, a press release!

What is a press release exactly? In a nutshell, a press release (or media release/alert) is typically a news-oriented document of varied length that is formatted specifically to read in a familiar, informative and effective manner. So, when anyone in the media receives and opens up a release, they should immediately know how the document will look, flow and quickly locate critical pieces of information without second-guessing. There isn't one "rulebook" for press releases, but most publicists and communications experts tend to stick with what works for the sake of respecting the media's time and preferred working style. A press release is typically written in the 3rd person, and should always be written about something important to the music media, public (fans) or general music industry. Examples being; album releases, a new single, a record deal, new manager, band breakup (it happens) etc.

A great press release should flow like a news piece, or as a reference to something you may read on one of your favorite websites about music. A release is usually written with the mindset that you would utilize for a college/high school essay, keeping rules of tight grammar and structure at the forefront. That doesn't mean you shouldn't have fun with it, especially if it's on-brand for what you're creating and would better capture interest. Remember this is just as much about grabbing attention as it is providing critical info for the reader. You can't have one without the other, as for example, you snag interest with the title, but the release misses information they would use in a confirmed article or even missing your contact information (yikes!).

Over the past 14 years, I have written hundreds of music-focused press releases, and while each one is different, I have developed a style that is my boilerplate for most releases I put into the world. However, I'm always researching and learning about ways to write a better, tighter and more appealing release. What the media would have appreciated and expected from me in 2007 is quite different from what I would send today. Not only is the media world more saturated in news and competitive, but the way we all communicate on a professional level has evolved and changed.

So, where does one start with writing a press release? In addition to whatever I recommend and draft out below for you, I always suggest doing your "homework" and looking at examples of other press releases you can find online. Believe me, they are out there and as a bonus, seek out the ones in the given genre of music you are working in. While there is a certain way to write, and <u>not</u> to write a press release, it's really nothing to pull your hair over since it's about the story and information, but not really about the length or the actual writing style. It's much better to give it a shot with limited wisdom than to never try and think you aren't deserving of media attention. It's always best to prepare, but for the sake of progress and growth, don't overthink this.

Okay, let's dive deeper. In the formal structure of a press release, you typically have the title, summary, body, boilerplate and footer containing critical contact information for yourself or whomever the primary contact is to be. As stated, the journey of writing a press release is ultimately up to you, but this format/order is one that I have used for many years and based on the work of major and independent press organizations this is used as well. To be safe though, stick with what you read below for starters and evolve as you get comfortable with the process.

Let's talk about length for a second. I highly recommend anyone reading this who is "new to the game" of being an artist and reaching out to the media to practice the art of brevity. Getting to the point, and keeping your outreach request and your press release short and sweet will increase the likelihood of a response. Since someone in the media may open your pitch or release out of curiosity, or even better, due to a genuine, well-written introduction, you now have a limited amount of time to keep their attention and win their commitment for coverage.

A short press release will still uphold the qualities of a longer one, whereas a long press release is typically reserved for someone with more tenure with the media, or perhaps for an artist who has been in the game for many years. Your press release will be a small fraction of the length of something coming from Post Malone, Metallica or Lil' Wayne's media team, make sense? Getting to the point in your title, summary and body will provide the information needed without diving into the realm of information overload. Believe me, if there's too much information some writers may say "screw it" and move on to something else, even if they were intending on covering your release. Simplicity is key, especially in today's distraction-filled society.

A mindset of gratitude is important, as your release is likely at the bottom of the totem pole of writer's tasks, so be sure to play nice, keep things short and be very thankful if the media bites on your pitch and press release. That's not a bad thing, but just how it works. We all start somewhere, and the rapport is built by becoming not only someone with great music, but also being someone the media loves to work with for many reasons. For example, "Sarah always responds quickly!", "John always gives me all the information upfront" or even "Kim is nice, hilarious and always brings me something awesome to cover".

Okay, let's get to it. Here's the basic structure of a press release in which you should practice writing, and even share with others in your circle for proof of grammar, structure and most importantly the quality of the content. Will it keep someone's interest? Will they find it compelling? Is it newsworthy? You get it, now let's break things down...

The Title - Believe it or not, this is absolutely the most important part of the press release. Think about it, you are strolling through a bookstore, perhaps without a set purchase in mind, and are browsing through thousands of books, magazines and even newspapers all around you. What captures your attention, perhaps the marketing of a great title on end caps or a book that simply stands out because of what topics you are into? We all have a limited attention span, especially in the world of media where journalists are bombarded with pitches hourly and when searching for content on specific assignments, usually go to their tried and tested sources (favorite publicists, bands/ artists already creating buzz, Google etc). The obvious first thing any media person reads on your release is that title, so make it sticky and something to remember.

While not necessary, above the title if you have an artist or company logo it's always helpful to add to the top. It helps cement your brand and reminds the reader whom the topic is about. Plus, if you have a cool logo, rock it!

The Summary - While typically reserved for the formatting needs of mass press aggregators like PR Newswire, the summary is meant to complete the brief synopsis of what the title is announcing. You shouldn't repeat any information in the summary that is in the title, but of course, you can always use this information in the body of the media release. For example, if the title is "Barking dog band releases howling new single bark the night away", the summary could be something like "The new track is set for a 11/11 release via cassette, vinyl and streaming sources including Spotify and Apple Music." Remember, the summary isn't always needed, but it's helpful especially if a media source is looking for as much information as quickly as possible.

The Body - This is the good stuff, the meat of the press release that compacts as much relevant, juicy information into a handful of paragraphs as possible. Think of this as being the summary you read on the back of a book, but not the entire book. The body should be written in a captivating manner, telling the reader about what's going on without putting them to sleep or wasting their time. There is no reason a good body of a release should go more than 2-3 paragraphs, unless as mentioned you are Billie Elish and are announcing tons of information about a worldwide tour, a new album, a whole line of merchandise, new hair colors and cramming all this into one release that needs 2 pages to do it in.

The body gives the media source enough information to write about you in their own words, and is used as a point of reference about that given topic. If information outside of the specific news is used, it should only be because excluding the info would provide better context. It is critical to put yourself in the shoes of the journalist or writer, so only contribute the information needed to make a potential feature work. Another thing to remember at the end of a release is the boilerplate, which is essentially a condensed biography about the artist.

When beginning the body of a press release, be sure to include the dateline. This is essentially the exact date and city/location of where the artist or event is located. An example of a dateline would be something like **"11.11.2020 (PORTLAND, OR) - "** and usually this introduction is kept in bold. The first sentence should be a repeat of what you are driving home in the title, but shouldn't be the same thing as the title.

To continue the use of my obnoxious summary example, for the body I would kick it off with something like "Barking Dog Band, the BARKY nominated quintet for album of the year, has announced their newest single "Bark the night away" for a November release". You can then delve into the specifics including the actual release date, why the single is special, who produced it and of course why the group is important to begin with.

Boilerplate - The boilerplate is an important section of your media release that nails down who the artist or band is. This section should ideally be no more than 3-5 sentences but in the music industry, the rules are a bit more flexible so it can also be a condensed version of your existing biography. While I feel an extensive biography in 2020 is a bit unnecessary and actually runs the chance of making you look silly, I do think a tight bio or boilerplate is a smart piece of information to keep on hand for media releases and more.

You can use the boilerplate on social media, one sheets and even in email pitches you send out for news, promotional, booking, management and other various reasons. Okay okay, I know you want to just see an example, so I have something for you below to copy/paste and edit to make it your own. Heck, that's what I would have done so here you go!

Barking Dog Band is a 5 piece synthwave/rap group from Portland, Oregon. Formed in 2018 and fronted by The Voice finalist Pit Bill, the eclectic group is rounded out by musicians who have performed with top-selling artists around the globe. The band is set to release their sophomore album 'In the doghouse' in December 2020 and is the follow-up to their 2018 debut EP. As one of Portland's top-drawing acts, the group is noted for their onstage antics, wall of sound energy and unique mixing of genres.

You get the vibe here, it's enough to understand where the band is from, what they sound like, what the latest news is and what the album(s) are called. Short, sweet and to the point. You're welcome.

Contact Information - Admittedly, I've left this information out quite a few times early in my career and I wondered why the lack of response was happening. If you have some great news and your press release ends up being shared with others or is posted online, most will look at the bottom (or top) of your press release to find out how to contact the party responsible.

It's good to at least include an email, but many also include a phone number if you have an office line. Do NOT put your cell phone number if you are posting this online, as you'll end up becoming the victim of more robocalls than you would ever imagine.

Additional information - For 99.9% of us, the press release will be created and distributed in a digital format including PDF, word, pasted into an email or even being hosted online in various ways. This goes into the importance of including links to critical bits of information relevant to your music news. If you have a new single, and it's out for public consumption, include the hyperlink in the press release in obvious to find areas. Not only is this great for SEO if hosted online, but it makes the lives of those reading it much easier.

Including photos or images on the release can be incredibly useful as well. Examples of that being a press photo of the artist/group, an image of the album/single cover, or an admat for a specific show or festival the artist is performing at. The exact image used in the release may need to be of a smaller file size if you choose to export the press release as a PDF, so we'll need to ensure you have these images (also known as media assets) available in a convenient location. You can host these on a specific media page on your website, attach them to your pitch email, link to them in the press release or simply offer them upon request when pitching. It's always wise to have them offered and available upfront, for obvious reasons.

For examples of press releases visit BradleyPublicity.com or search "press release examples" on Google. Remember, there is not a one size fits all solution for press releases.

10. How to pitch the media (and actually get a response)

Let's dive into one of the most critical elements of the book, and note that absolutely none of the previous material matters unless you truly grasp the point in this chapter. This is extremely sensitive because each individual in the media is...are you ready for it?...a unique human just like you and I. However, those who work in the media do adhere to certain rules and expectations when it comes to doing their jobs day to day. Compared to other industries and careers that may require predictable and standard talents across the board, public relations is an interesting blend of sales, marketing and often complicated tiers of administration.

Each relationship you create with the media should be treated professionally, but especially in music, so let's avoid sending those robotic-sounding emails or showing up for meetings dressed in a suit. It's 2020, who does that anyway?? I'm going to shoot straight here, taking the right route when pitching the media will be ten times more time-consuming than taking the quick, painless route which I'll explain more about. Often we feel pressed for time and want to just get this done, but don't let that get the best of you by making decisions that you later regret.

I'm not trying to discourage you or looking to chase anyone away in this chapter but I do have to lay down the rules so you can get into a solid mindset. One that is built around quality relationships and selling yourself in a way that comes off honest and genuine. All musicians think that their music is the best thing in the world and that it deserves all the attention possible. That is perfectly normal and believe me, I have felt the same way about my own music as well, but when it comes to dealing with the media you want to avoid sounding entitled at all costs. The media can make or break your perception with the public and you have to put aside your ego and think clearly with all outreach.

What really matters when putting together that pitch and gearing up to send that first email is understanding that when you're first getting started your efforts are as personal and customized as possible. I'll be honest, I had to learn part of this the hard way, and I promise you that sending 10 emails to 10 different people that are from the heart with a genuine interest in what they do will go over so much better than a hundred emails that come from a robot. This isn't bashing mailing lists by the way, and I will address that separately. I know I know we don't have the time for these personalized emails, but believe me, when they see your robotic email without a proper introduction, don't expect a response 99% of the time. The preparation for pitching to Media is just as important as when you actually pull the trigger and get started on pitching.

So where do we start? First off, write the tried and tested phrase "Keep it Simple" and put it on a sticky note by your computer. Think about it this way, if you were to receive an email from somebody and it was six paragraphs long with so much information that it makes your head spin you'd probably delete the message or would wait a couple of days (or even weeks) in your inbox before you got around to it. The secret is keeping the messaging simple, well-written and so easy to understand that your ten-year-old could get a grasp on what you have to offer. I know that's frustrating to some because you want to give them all the information all at once, but that's what a press release and having a separate resource folder (media assets) helps with. That folder may include a Media Kit, one sheet, photos, artwork and other things that will help them put together their features if they are interested. The goal here is to get in the door with these individual media contacts and build that initial relationship and interest first.

So I challenge you. Once you start putting together your very first pitch and getting a vibe for how you want to communicate with the media, write those first messages but take an hour or two away from it to let it sink in. I'm not asking you to be the typical musician that second-guesses themselves and takes decades to finish an album (haha), I just imply that you take a step back, look at this scenario again and think to yourself "will this get me the response that I am looking for?". When the person on the other side of the email opens up your message, anything more than a paragraph runs the high risk of being ignored or simply put on the back burner until that person has downtime. However, believe me, these people get hundreds of emails and don't have a free moment till the holidays (not kidding, this feels like a 24/7 job for many of us sometimes).

Piecing together your first pitch, which I stress should be unique and tailored for each contact, should have the basic type of greeting that you would use introducing yourself to someone at a business networking event or to a music executive at a show. You want to convey that you're not just trying to knock down their door and more so asking "hey is it okay if I connect with you?" while ensuring you respect their valuable time. This will break the ice and put the ball in their court. It will give that person the feeling it's their decision to respond and if they want to help you the dynamic will be so much better. Secondly, when you reach out to somebody in the media, show some proof that you understand what they cover and why it would be of interest to them.

For example, you play in an awesome jazz fusion band based out of Tampa and you find a great writer that's perfect because they covered one of your favorite bands that happens to be in the same genre. Your first outreach might be something like "Hey Sally, I really connected with that review that you did for XYZ band in last month's issue. The writing and insight really impressed me and I'm glad that you also like one of my favorite bands. I wanted to reach out to you, introduce myself and see if it's okay to pitch you some music from my band." Something of that tone and brevity shows that you actually care, and took the time to know who you're reaching out to set a vibe for the conversation knowing you have something to ask of them. 99% of the time you'll get a response or at least you'll get respect from that individual out of that conversation.

Don't be offended if your outreach goes unanswered, but know that more than likely they appreciated the note because you are showing respect and admiration for work they often do for a living. We all love a little validation and a good compliment now and then, right? Imagine if someone comes up to you at a show and tells you how much they appreciated your set or your album, how does that make you feel? Pretty good right? So, put yourself in the shoes of a fan and as someone with a business mindset that is ready to carefully sell a creative product to somebody willing to listen.

11 - Show and tour promotion

The funny thing about being in a band or being a musician is that the amount of prep work is about equal for both a multiple week-long tour or just one local show. I always think about that fact when speaking with my own friends that I play music with and my clients. Sometimes that's just the right amount of incentive to push yourself to hit the road and play shows outside of your local area (*or comfort zone*).

I completely understand the behind-the-scenes work can be extremely time-consuming and stressful. Especially when you're balancing other things such as family, work and even children. For those that are younger and reading this book, you have the most opportunity out of all of us to maximize some of these tips regarding live shows and tour promotions.

So you booked your next show, congratulations and that's half the battle right there. Making the effort to do the networking, relationship building with talent bookers and getting the people you play music with together to commit to this event. There are some no-brainer things that we all do to prepare for the show, like calling our friends, posting on Facebook, and maybe throwing up some posters at the local venue if the talent booker and staff don't do so on their own. Some of these thoughts straddle the line between public relations and traditional marketing, so give me a pass in this section.

I come from an era where I was signed to many labels and helped build our own band (brand) from the ground up with some amazing bandmates. It took putting certain steps into play that worked out in our favor. Ever since my touring and days of being a professional artist I have helped hundreds of other artists carve their own path with my marketing/PR services and below are some common themes that just seemed to work a lot of the time. Of course there is luck and solid relationships that always help, but for the rest of us the hard work really does pay off if you have great music and a solid mindset to get s*** done.

Local Shows - Whether you have played no shows or a hundred, listen up. Now is the time to take an honest assessment and audit of the efforts that you take to promote the upcoming shows with your band. Break out a piece of paper or use a notes app on your computer or phone, and list out the things that you do to promote the show(s) that you have lined up.

After you're done and before reading on, I want you to think about this and ask yourself, do you think these things will bring heads into the venue to come see your band? Be honest with yourself here and think about the things that are working and the ones that maybe you should step up on. They're also things that maybe you had no idea you could do to promote your band, and we'll dive into that. I'm sure many who are reading this already know about all these things, but an amazing part of learning and growing is to be reminded of what works and what we can always improve upon.

Now, remember public relations is the perception that the general public and your fans will ultimately come to regarding your brand or band. Much of these efforts are filtered through the media so you have to make sure that your messaging and information is tied together nicely and easy to understand. This is why it is important to make a list of what it is that you're going to do to promote each and every upcoming show that you have. Planning will help you hold yourself accountable, execute and reach the targets that will best serve your band.

Social Networking - let's start with the obvious ones, Facebook, Instagram and all other relevant social media channels that the majority are using at the time of reading. I'm trying to keep this book Evergreen, as sometimes I have read business books that have tried and tested principles but then they start talking about Myspace and other platforms that immediately makes what I'm reading seem incredibly dated. I'm sure the first thing that you will do is make a post on Facebook and Instagram, perhaps of the flyer, letting people know that you have a show coming up and telling them "hey come hang out, grab a beer". But then 90% of the time I see zero information with ticket links, incentives and other fine important details that would push me over the edge to come to that show.

Facebook and Instagram run on algorithms that are typically not friendly towards external links or things that seem promotional. This is why it's important to allocate a small but realistic budget towards boosting posts when promoting events such as upcoming local shows. This also applies to album and single promotions, pretty much in the same format. The beauty part of Facebook and Instagram is that it lets you hyper-target by region and even demographics and interests. So, if you were playing a show in downtown Tulsa, you can run Facebook ads that only go out to music fans of your specific genre that live within say 5 miles of downtown. You don't want to run the ad and have it go to everyone around the world or the country, as that would be wasting money and you want to spend it wisely. Now, more than ever it's easier to spend advertising money and get it as close as possible to the right kind of people that would appreciate your live show. I am not an SEO expert and don't do a lot with advertising but this is a critical part of promoting your shows on social media.

Other ideas that you can put into action include contests, exclusive merchandise previews and developing content that is consistent and engaging that will help keep your upcoming show on the radar of your current and potential new fans. It's ultimately up to you to brainstorm and create the type of content that best fits your audience as I could write an entire book full of ideas that apply to different types of artists, genres and regions.

The idea is to actually take steps that go beyond simply posting that you have a show coming up on social media and taking things a step further. Make sure your content makes people stop scrolling even if it's for a few seconds. I recently went to a show down the street for a band that I truly enjoy and honestly I probably wouldn't have gone if it wasn't for the reasonably priced VIP package that got me a vinyl, laminate and chance to meet the band for a few minutes. I know that's a bit of an extreme in comparison to an emerging artist, but great ideas are transferable and could be applied in a way that works best for you.

Real-life networking - It's true that you don't have to leave your keyboard to effectively promote your upcoming show. The naysayers may criticize us but we're living in a digital world where live streaming, social media outlets can get the word out faster than anyone could in person. That being said, if you have the ability to carve out time to go to a couple shows a week or even a month to show your face, make some friends and further build your professional contacts, I promise you that your shows will have more in attendance. The reasons should be obvious. People, including us music fans, can only retain so much information and plan for so many things. The things that we end up doing usually come from the ideas that are top of mind, and that typically originates from friends, word-of-mouth, social media, websites and even print media. Think about the last few places that you went to enjoy yourself, especially a show, how did you find out about them? Reverse-engineer that thought process and try that yourself. It just may work.

So, specifically regarding going to shows, especially ones that are in a genre similar to yours. I'm talking about the kind where the audience may appreciate what you're doing. Make sure you are proactive about letting everyone you run into about what you're up to musically. One way to do that, which applies to almost anything in life, is to first stop asking anyone that you're talking with to help. First, ask them what are they up to, how are they doing, how is life going?

Showing genuine interest for those in your community will in turn lead to them asking what you are up to. That will then give you the chance to tell them about the show that you have and you have the permission to invite them. The reason I mention this is that people hate being marketed to in any forceful way, but people enjoy meeting others that have a genuine interest in them. Almost always, in the conversation they will return the favor and ask "so what do you do, how are you?" which then you drop the info on your music.

Unless you were handing out flyers at the end of the show, which I suggest you still do because nobody does it anymore, I strongly urge you to take the approach of getting to know as many people at shows as possible. It's just important to do it in a way that doesn't obviously come off like you have some sort of shameless self-promotional agenda. I also hope that you were doing your due diligence of getting to know the decision-makers at the actual venue, and offering to do whatever it takes to help the venue promote your show, which will make them want to promote you as much as possible. This all ties together because venues typically run ads in local print media and post events and ads online. The work that you do as an artist or band simply amplifies the efforts and everyone will be happy when there are more heads in the room.

Media outreach - At least 2-3 weeks out from your show it would best serve you to put together a press release or at piece together a brief but informative email that you can send to regional media about your upcoming event. You want to include obvious details including door time, show start, what bands are playing, cost of entry, age limit, and what's special about the headliner. This press release should have all of these details neatly organized with links to pre-sale ticket information and the venue website so every journalist can decide if they would like to cover your show. There is no guarantee that the media will cover your show, as this is a fiercely competitive market even for large major label artists. There are more shows per week especially in major cities than you could ever imagine.

So the goal here is to build those solid relationships and send pitches to the right media contacts about your show that are quick and easy to read and get to the point about why your show is worth their time. If you pitch someone too far out, they may forget about it or if you catch it too close to the events, you may have missed your window and they already have commitments to coverage elsewhere that night. Things to include when pitching the press on your upcoming show are the same as if you were pitching your new album or single, that would include a press photo, bio, link to your music, and of course all of the relevant information about the show.

In a way, the regional press game is a bit easier than promoting a new single or album, simply because there are fewer contacts to deal with. However, on the same note, it often feels more difficult because you have more competition since there are fewer writers and sources covering local shows. If you live in a major city or region, you will also be facing competition with other shows that same week or even that same night. If that is the case, it's good to manage expectations as there is a chance your show simply may not make the cut. It's nothing personal, and editors only have so much room for so many shows.

One of two things will likely happen if someone in the media agrees to cover your show. They will likely send out one to two contacts and one most likely will be a photographer. You want to make sure that the concert venue is looped in on any media guest that may be attending your show with specifics like if they are bringing a camera to take photos or video. Some venues may have very specific regulations for or against video and photos, and even for listing media in the first place.

That's why I stress having great relationships with your talent bookers in venues so they will want to help you when it comes to tasks such as media and guest lists. I always suggest getting a media list to the venue at least a couple days ahead of the show. Compare the guest list for friends and family which usually are due at check-in. These are small details I know, but if you get in a good habit of preparing people ahead of time, I promise you these venues will like you a lot more than others that aren't prepared.

If you happen to have no luck getting media to come to your event there are proactive ways for you to secure post-show coverage. One of those is a friend or hired professional taking your own photos and videos of the set. The better the quality, the better the chance you'll have at pitching these for post-show coverage. This strategy will work better for artists that at least have somewhat of a name or buzz locally or at least a relationship existing with local media. In many cities, there always seems to be at least one or two websites that cover music that often cover live shows.

Tour promotion - I purposely saved this section to be last, because all of the rules above apply and tour promotion is simply on a much larger scale. This is where I highly suggest you get as organized as possible. Like breakout that spreadsheet and create tabs for each city of your tour, create your targets, do your research on media sources and pitch in the same way I suggested above. Yes, it's a lot more work and professionals and those at record labels are paid well to do this kind of work because it is time-consuming.However,

I promise it is very much worth your time to spend an equal block of time preparing, pitching and following up for each and every city that you have on your upcoming track. This could make the difference between well-attended shows and empty rooms, and even more important the ongoing growth of your music career.

12 - How to protect your reputation

Perhaps this chapter should have been placed closer to the beginning of this book, but I'm writing in a bit of a freeflow format based on ideas that have come to mind over the past few months of putting this together. I have been coming and going into this book as I work with my awesome PR clients so it's really something that is in real-time and based off of the real-life situations I have to manage on a daily basis.

Maintaining my own reputation as a publicist is just as important as helping build those for my clients. PR and marketing is always a work in progress and is not an exact science. It has no guarantees and every artist and professional is going to have a unique experience with this process. That being said, a reputation is simply the perception and opinion that others have of you based on what current and cumulative information they have about your music and brand.

Some artists are very outspoken, outgoing and are willing to do anything to catch that buzz and stay on people's radars. On the flip side, some artists are quite introverted, don't care what people think about them, and are sometimes hesitant to pursue media coverage and even promote what they're doing to the general public.

Everyone loves positive attention and validation for what they're doing, but sometimes artists get attention for things that are negative and it could be a really hard pill to swallow. There's the saying "any PR is good PR", and a lot of the times I actually agree with that because things come and go so quickly that people forget about the little f*** ups just as they eventually forget about positive news. If it makes the news and you didn't kill somebody, sometimes you have to remember that's keeping you top-of-mind with listeners and the media. Take this at face value, and as I said every artist's situation is different and is always a case by case scenario.

Planning out how you want to be perceived by the media, the public and your fans is something you should consider and keep top of mind if you have plans of making a career in music. This is a very broad topic as what one artist is known for may be the polar opposite of what you actually want to be known for. For example, say an artist in hard rock wants to be known for extreme fashion, crazy live shows and stirring the pot with drama, that's not always a bad thing and that can lead to a lot of press on top of the coverage of music.

Another artist, say a reserved singer-songwriter type, wants to be known for their philanthropy and giving back because they care about a cause very deeply. Anytime you see these positive "tug at the heartstring" stories in the media about your favorite artist, a lot of the time it was sparked by a publicist or intentionally sent to the media from the actual artist. It's good to take credit for the things that you want to be known for, especially if it's something that is helping the greater good of music and humankind.

I'll address crisis PR with urgent situations shortly, but this chapter is focused specifically on maintaining your desired reputation during consistent, good times. Each time that you make a post on social media, have a conversation on stage with your audience and even with fans and journalists during interviews at the show, it all adds up to your general reputation. The average music fan typically gravitates towards musicians and groups that have either impeccable reputations or those that are known for edgy behavior or sometimes those whose career is currently a train wreck (any TMZ fans here?). As long as nobody gets hurt, I leave the reputation building to the artist with a strict note to always remember that every move made and word that can be found online or on video is adding up to equal your unique reputation.

The great part about being a musician is that music fans love a great story and want to hear about things good and bad with the artists they follow. Being candid, honest and forthcoming about both challenging and amazing victories in your career is something that is highly appreciated in today's music media. It is true that in decades past, artists were a bit more cryptic, but there are many factors that just don't apply today including lack of social media and more control over conversations by print media and record labels. There were simply more gatekeepers, less overall artists, less online media and this all added up to reputations being much easier to maintain and control.

Today, from the second an artist begins making their persona public, that artist should be mindful that anything and everything can be used against them in the "court of social media." One day you may just do something that ends up getting 12 million views in 48 hours and you didn't even see it coming. Or, you may be climbing your way in your career and all of a sudden something you said in an interview or on social media from a couple of years back comes back to haunt you.

Plan your communications - I understand the idea of preparing how you communicate with anyone outside of your internal team and bandmates may seem super uncomfortable. However, planning ahead on your tone and messaging for everything you will put into the world may be one of the best decisions you ever make. This book obviously won't teach you how to write your content, but if you need guidance on what specific content to include in your social media calendars and media releases, study online content posted by artists and professionals you admire the most.

The more you educate yourself and write as a tool of communication with your fans and the media, especially by studying those who are already successful, the quicker you will see results with your fans and ultimately with the media as you build relationships with them. This is not saying you must write like a novelist or a reporter at the newspaper, but more so stressing that you develop a style that is authentic to your brand but also effectively gets the point across. As you begin securing more press with the media, these people will be watching your social media and blog postings, and there will be a chance that the media will pick up your news, content and even pull quotes from what you post. This is why planning and proofing your content is so critical.

Before you post any blogs or finalize your social media posts, be sure to take a step back and revisit your content to check for grammar, structure and ensure the right information is included for whatever it is you want to push. For those that don't know, a social media calendar can be your best friend, and is a planned out document that contains all the social media copy and links to images you choose to include in upcoming posts. You can then easily schedule these posts natively on social media or create reminders to refer to this document so your social posts are consistent and remain on-brand. There's nothing wrong with a spontaneous post, but sometimes those are the ones that lead to regretful decisions if they are done during times of stressful situations. If you think what you're about to post may have a polarizing effect, take a moment to plan it out, take a short break and then revisit and decide if it's your best decision.

Audit your presence - As time goes on, you'll want to consistently audit your controlled online territory (social media, blogs, completed interviews etc) as well as content about your brand written by others. Tools like Google Alerts can help you easily keep track of any new content posted online in real-time. Search engines can quickly help you filter and locate existing content for you to review and take action if necessary. Sometimes you will find content that needs updated facts, or even something you will need to dispute if it shines you in a negative light.

It's also a good idea to scroll through your social media channels like Facebook, Instagram and Twitter to check and make sure your content stays relevant to your brand and stands the test of time. I'll let you decide what works and what doesn't, but if any part of you feels specific content may trigger a red flag to someone in the media, it may be a good idea to remove or edit that content. Remember, those in the media who want to cover your music will usually Google you and look you up on popular social media channels. Put yourself in their shoes and decide if what they find may help them make a positive or negative judgement about your reputation.

Prepare for the what-ifs - Take into consideration all things good and bad that may come your way as an artist. Regardless of whether the media covers your latest music or events, you should always be prepared for the unexpected and sometimes the inevitable. To keep things positive, usually, it's when something fantastic that happens to an artist is when opportunities are lost. For example, say your new single gets played on local radio, or a huge blog does a writeup on you soon after finding your music on Spotify. What do you do?? This is where having the preparation work sorted out for those "what if" moments. Avoid being a deer in the headlights and you can then spring into action with that PR mindset to secure more opportunities.

Of course, it's not possible to be ready for everything, just as the music world wasn't ready for COVID-19 when it suddenly changed everything. A good PR mindset involves being open-minded and ready to pivot when things are most uncomfortable and uncertain. This not only applies to relationships in the media, but your overall relationships with fans and music enthusiasts you can and should stay connected with. This all ties together, and always being ready with a strategy, response and proactive approach to your brand marketing will set your music career up for consistent growth.

Let's consider a potentially negative situation. Perhaps you said something online about another artist or genre of music that didn't go over well long-term. You're up for a great show or a tour and someone on earth could easily derail the opportunity. As mentioned before, don't stay quiet unless it's absolutely necessary. If you are not clear about something that could be a detriment to your career, it's time to put your PR mindset into action with a brief pause, planning a quick response that is vulnerable and professionally planned. These steps will help you react in a way that asks for forgiveness which is actually believable. There's a fine line between casually handling small situations that may look bad or potentially foolish, and those scenarios that fall into the crisis category mostly handled by professionals. The more you progress through your career in music, you may run into a little of both to some degree. The point is to be prepared and to not let these things derail your progress over the long haul. I like to believe with anything that if you make mistakes, you are actually doing something right because you are actually trying. Try not to make the same mistake twice though, hah!

13 - Crisis management for artists

I really had to think hard about this before taking the plunge on this chapter. The idea of crisis management as a broad range topic makes most of us think of large corporations and those facing unprecedented challenges, jaw-dropping mistakes, social media slip-ups, lawsuits and management shake-ups. In the world of creative arts, including all us musicians reading this, once in a blue moon, a challenge may arise that could spell the potential end of a career. However, these issues likely pale in comparison to those faced by large corporations which can cost thousands of jobs, millions of dollars, lost sales and a destroyed brand. If a company drops the ball and faces a media crisis, they often hire an entire communication team to help protect their brand in the face of that given crisis.

Thankfully, for the majority of artists even the largest of problems and challenges can be handled swiftly by the actual artist, manager, record label or of course the public relations rep they happen to be working with. Obviously, this book helps cover the DIY approach to public relations so let's take a closer look at how a PR crisis may be handled so you have a bit more perspective on what I'm talking about.

In my almost 20 years of being an artist, touring endlessly and finally jumping on the other side of the desk to work with artists in different capacities, I've witnessed almost every type of problem that an artist can run into. Starting with an example that is sometimes unavoidable or likely not the fault of an artist (such as a cancelled tour) the situation should always be handled like a PR pro. Especially if you want to yield the best outcome for those disappointed fans and those involved. A cancelled tour, or even a local show is usually a scenario that can have a negative effect on your fans, the talent buyer and even the other artists on that show if you are the headliner.

To clarify on this topic, crisis management in PR is both something that is proactive and reactive. Sometimes one is simply trying to clean up a mess that has already occurred, and other times efforts are made to communicate a point proactively before the media and general public discover X issue from another source. Acting swiftly to deliver the bad news for something like this mentioned cancelled show or tour should be done in a vulnerable way that comes off honest and apologetic. People need the details neatly laid out, and if you avoid sounding like a robot you will usually earn sympathy and ongoing respect.

You've seen it before locally for sure, a show gets cancelled but you hear about it through the grapevine but see nothing online from the artist. It can often lead to disappointment, confusion and a bad reputation if the artist happened to have interest from the media on that given date. All of the buzz, conversations that happen around these types of situations are part of your reputation, your brand and ultimately your relationships with those who can help you (managers, labels, magazines, blogs, other artists etc).

Going silent and forgetting to update your social media and any relevant media about this change of event status can put you in a pile of s*** for not giving appropriate parties a heads-up and giving all a chance to make other plans. This is especially relevant if you had media coverage confirmed for the upcoming show or tour. With a proper update, any media that is live online about your upcoming show can then be updated which will further help spread the important message, which can also include information on rescheduled dates or refunds.

The odd timing of this chapter just happens to align with an astronomical change of well...everything in this country. By the time you read this, I hope that Coronavirus is a thing of the past and is simply a learning opportunity for how artists and of course people in all types of business deal with major scenarios such as a pandemic, especially in such a tech-driven society. As most of us reading this know, within a week or two much of the touring industry was nearly wiped out for 2020. This was a major challenge for many in the industry on all sides of touring and promotions. Many were shocked and potentially put in financial ruin, but still left with the responsibility of communicating cancellations, refunds, credits and any sort of rescheduling accommodations that could be made.

These event-based companies and artists not only lost income, but were also responsible for taking the time (often without pay) to craft proper messaging to the media, industry professionals and of course to social media channels to deliver the bad news to fans. This type of Crisis Management in PR and media communications is obviously not ideal, and a lot of the time spent is extra hours out of your day to make things right. On a micro-level, going back to your cancelled show, a disappointed artist may not make the effort to inform people of the axed event as it may not seem like much of a big deal. However, I can assure you that this decision to make the effort will form into habits that you will have as your career grows. Those that you communicate with will remember how you handled yourself during great times and terrible times.

Okay here's another example, perhaps some sort of altercation, "artist beef" or even an issue with an internal band member occurs that lands them in trouble with the law or even on the front page of music news sources. I know these situations may be an extreme, but these things happen in all genres of music, all the time. What's funny though, most of the time what comes off as drama or what seems to be a major issue ends up working out in the long run. These issues end up getting media coverage on one or both sides, and ultimately give extra exposure to the artist(s). I'm not trying to give you any ideas here though.

This segways into issues where a legal council needs to be involved. If there's a chance the media also needs to be informed or if the news sites are already covering the subject it may be wise to run all communications by your lawyer first. This protects a sensitive situation from getting worse by saying the wrong thing, but also can avoid further legal issues by keeping all statements non-incriminating. Before anyone reading this book takes any of this advice and happens to be in a legal bind, I absolutely ask that you call your legal counsel before putting anything online or out to the media.

Every situation is different and you must learn to go with your gut on what feels right and determine what may not be a good use of your time. This is something to master so you can best protect your brand and leverage situations to shine you in the best possible light. We've all heard "there's no such thing as bad PR", which is honestly true most of the time. Media and the public tend to forget about most issues when nobody is hurt or loses a ton of money, but it's about how you approach the situation that can maximize your PR coverage and ensure you get to tell your side of the story.

Perhaps something happens to you or one of your band collaborators that may put your reputation in jeopardy. I'm thinking of the worst types of scenarios like if your bass player robbed a bank, like something that could potentially wipe out your sales and never get you back on tour ever again.

Communicating with people including your fans and the media will help avoid the rumor mill and potential issues with assumptions from spreading rampantly. The best type of solution is to prepare a statement that can be posted on social media and delivered to online and print media quickly. This provides an immediate offense and provides critical information for those who are interested. If the situation is dire, always run your communications by an actual professional or lawyer for an added layer of reputation protection.

Also, in most scenarios I can't stress enough that staying quiet is not a good look. It's usually a last resort, say if something stupid was mentioned that made the artist look bad, but was forgivable and needed time to wear off. Things can and will sometimes come back to haunt you, so proceed with your steps carefully. During and after a PR crisis, every chess move you make is traceable, usable against you and can lead to a desired or terrible outcome. These are the times to strategize, but while moving as quickly as possible to give the perception that you are taking the situation seriously.

I can promise you that even though it may seem like you're bringing more attention to something negative, this is more of a rip the Band-Aid off solution and doing it slowly is not the best way to stay on top of the problem. This advice applies to almost any type of issue that an artist may have, but remember every scenario is unique and case by case. For example, sometimes artists run into situations where one band member was the issue and to fix the problem they simply let the person go, followed with a prompt media alert to address and update their fans along with the press.

I won't go into any other examples in the real world but sometimes artists do things that are unforgivable and the best way to earn fan and public trust is for that person to go away. By the way, did I mention that going away for a while is also a great PR strategy if you do something foolish? Sometimes, though, that well-crafted apology and begging for forgiveness is just enough to help fix your PR image if the wound is still fresh.

If some of the advice that I've mentioned still doesn't work, maybe "going off the radar" and staying clear of social and mainstream media for a while just might help.

I'm sure you can think of many examples of celebrities and musicians who have taken this route and things have worked out fine in the long term. While I can't stress that every situation is unique, it is typically true that time heals most wounds. This holds especially true to negative coverage by the media in most scenarios.

Okay, I'll stop jumping into hypothetical situations and break this down into something that could be used as a checklist next time you or somebody in your network runs into a problem and it may look bad for the artist brand.

Designate the representative - Own up to it, swallow your pride and be prepared to completely take responsibility for whatever it is that has happened. Whatever you do, do not play any sort of blame games, vent on social media or turn into a four-year-old child looking for a pity party. If you're reading this and you have a crisis management situation on your hands, obviously I have no idea what it is that you did, but it's up to you to take a huge breath and take these steps to avoid further turmoil.

It's important to fully understand what it is that happened and be prepared to answer any sort of questions that may come your way after a statement is made. If you are a solo artist, then you've got to do this yourself, but if you're in a band it's best to appoint the person that deals with stress like a rockstar and has the time to create this messaging and also fill inquiries.

Get a strategy - This is where you sit down and either think to yourself or speak amongst your bandmates about how you want to handle this in the most professional manner possible. If it's something as simple as a cancelled tour, you want to think of what it is that you're going to say that explains why it was cancelled, what you will do to fix any sort of outstanding issues, and whether they will be rescheduled dates.

Prepare your messaging - Be sure to take the time to craft messaging that is honest, vulnerable and informative. Whether this is in the form of a press release or simply messaging that goes on social media, this stuff is permanent and once fans and the general public get their eyes on it, it's kind of hard to take it back. If you are in a group with other members, I suggest collaborating and getting the green light from all involved. If you have a manager, legal counsel or even a label, get those second opinions, especially if the matter is a potential big deal. I leave this up to you but I always suggest to be cautious and triple check what you put online and on socials.

Plan who you are targeting - The messaging should be directed towards who may be affected the most in the situation. In this book and industry, it's most likely the fans and/or professionals that keep the music industry wheels turning. A voice and tone that comes off like it is written for them specifically will help much more than writing something robotic that could be applied to any type of situation. If the situation is regional, include media copy that calls out the area, people involved and even venues to show that you are acknowledging those that are affected and give them a direct message that may include solutions, apologies or simply bits of information to keep them informed.

Keep an eye on the situation - If the situation is something that involves media and social activity, it's important to keep an eye on it daily and engage in the conversation only if absolutely necessary. There is a difference here between staying aware about conversations about your band, and actually getting involved with those giving feedback directly.

While writing this book there was a certain band that I actually worked with that was going through a PR nightmare in which the band was engaging directly with every possible fan and critic via social media and blogs directly. This is typically not the way to handle a crisis scenario, and honestly it has hurt the band's reputation immensely. However, it has kept them in the news so this would be an example of "there's no such thing as bad PR" (even though there is).

When I say keep an eye on something, it's more for the purpose of knowing what is going on day to day so you can be prepared to deal with the media and any other involved parties when necessary. Whether you're dealing with legal counsel, management, your label or just handling things internally, being aware of the general online dialogue will help you handle the situation without being ignorant. As you track these conversations throughout the week, refer to the steps above to deal with them accordingly.

Learn from all issues - During this situation and in the timeframe immediately following the crisis, it is good to take a period of reflection to learn about what happened and how it ultimately affected you. Usually a PR crisis is something one would like to avoid happening a second time, and it's always a positive to make the changes that ensure this. Every scenario is typically different, but as humans we are designed to learn from mistakes but not all are that lucky and sometimes become repeat offenders. It's a good practice to have a purposeful conversation about the PR crisis to list out those changes to ensure it never goes down again.

14 - PR stunts

I'm sure we can think of a million PR stunts that have become iconic due to the sheer genius and "wow factor" of how they actually pulled it off. Those that make the most impact can cement the legacy of the brand, while other attempts can make people look foolish or even worse, desperate. For artists, it's the dream of everyone involved to drum up a plan that will help turn heads and make the news. From Lady Gaga's infamous sporting of a meat dress at an award show to random bands stopping freeway traffic to throw an impromptu show, some artists are willing to try anything to get coverage. I'm all for thinking up wild ideas and executing, but some circumstances will come with a risk.

In a crowded music space and with media being bombarded with record labels, artists, and even managers trying to get in their ears, sometimes a good PR stunt is just the right way to land on their radar without going direct every single time. Not all PR stunts are obviously the same, and the agenda will always differ situation by situation. Most fall under the tag of "creative marketing" to garner fan and media attention while others launch bold ideas that risk falling flat, earning worthy buzz or worse case, garnering negative coverage as the end result. The best outcomes usually come with careful planning, research and being bold while assessing positive and negative consequences.

Many of us remember in 2014 when the rock band U2 put their music on our iPhones and iPods (remember those?) without any sort of permission. While the band had all the right intentions and did this without any expectation of compensation, the campaign faced massive backlash for many reasons. This PR stunt indeed gained much press exposure, a huge win actually, but was lambasted for invading people's privacy by appearing on our most personal piece of technology without permission. At the time most people had 8GB phones, and the last thing people wanted is for some band they may or may not like taking up more room on their phone. There could be so many other reasons, but this broke the rule of Malcolm Gladwell's famed 'Permission Marketing'. This was indeed non-traditional marketing, but, securing that crucial permission in advance from the fan was not given.

An example of a PR stunt gone right goes back decades, with the Beatles playing their famed final show on the rooftops of Apple Corps (not the computer company) in 69' for adoring fans and soon after winning worldwide media buzz. It also helped that they were the biggest band in the world, but remember that ideas are transferable and scalable. Nobody forced their fans to attend, as many had no idea of the plans and soon after those who were tastemakers spread the word like a wildfire internationally. Not only did the media pick up the news, but fans and music enthusiasts alike have continued to tell the tale of that fateful day for almost 50 years. While an independent artist may not make an impact like The Beatles did, it's worth noting that a well-executed idea can place you on the map and build some well-deserved recognition.

Other occurrences of often carefully planned stunts include rockstar relationships, which I hate to burst your bubble but sometimes with celebrities they are not genuine and are used to gain press for each individual brand. Artist "beef", especially in rock and hip-hop can often be planned ahead of time to create media coverage and get communities talking (or even arguing). An immediate thought in recent history was Machine Gun Kelly and Eminem, which probably wasn't the best campaign involving artist beef manufactured for press, but it ultimately still got both artists a ton of press. Sometimes these stunts can be painfully obvious to the average fan, and other times they have no clue and they get away with it looking like the effort was 100% organic. These situations are typically low risk to the artist's brand, and the polarizing and viral conversations they develop is ultimately the desired result.

Over the years there has been every type of PR stunt imaginable pulled off with massive benefits for the artist, including retail activations, social media takeovers, contests and exclusive press features that leak precious information that ends up spreading online. The truth is that most things you see about a notable artist in the press were planned, unless it's something negative where they risk going to jail or something of a potentially criminal level.

Management and PR plan ahead for ways for their artists to secure organic coverage and viral buzz via social media, and in today's oversaturated media climate, it's often a must. For independent artists, sometimes you need more than quality reviews and interviews to get to where you need in your career. Success from PR stunts relies most often on the best creative thinking, original ideas and dipping into the pool of proven campaigns that have worked for others.

So, for your first PR stunt be mindful of these steps if you don't remember anything else. Make sure this creative marketing idea is planned out, studied online for other examples and executed only when you feel all your ducks are in a row. Are you ready for any type of outcome? Are you ready to push the news to the media channels if it catches a wave? As with anything in PR and marketing, there's no guarantee of results and it's usually better to have tried than to wonder in retrospect what could have been. Tread lightly on marketing risks that could land you in trouble, or make you or someone else look foolish. That being said, this is where I also recommend having friends and mentors in the world of marketing, so you can bounce these ideas off them for feedback.

15 - Databases and contact management

As you move along your journey developing your relationship with the media and reaching out to different contacts, you'll run into a situation that most of us have to deal with in any type of industry. Where do we put all these contacts? Also, where do we put in notes about these contacts or interactions so we know where we left off and what those little details are that really matter to building that relationship? Most of us forget little things very easily as time goes on, so we take notes in different ways and keep track of contact information similarly.

Most of us are familiar with contact software that is included in programs such as Microsoft Outlook, Gmail or contact managers that are built into our computers like on this MacBook I'm writing this book on. At the least, I highly recommend keeping track of the email and name of the people that you reach out to so you don't run into a situation where you forget it and have no idea where you put it.

Digging through emails can be laborious and often emails are deleted by accident or misplaced due to not remembering what to search for when looking for that contact. We've all been in that scenario where somebody was talking to ask us hey what's your email again or hey what's your phone number? We then roll our eyes and think why didn't you just take it down so you remember. I'd like to at least feel important enough that the people I deal with would keep track of my information somehow.

What I have found over the years is that a lot of publicists use spreadsheets to keep track of contacts and to report on the progress they have when reaching out to the media. Some spreadsheets are free like with this MacBook and with other programs like Google Docs, which can be found with a quick search on Google. These programs are incredibly easy to use and are actually very robust, allowing you to create different column automation tabs to make your life as easy as possible with all of your contacts.

Once you get in the habit of taking notes on your contacts and conversations, I promise you'll feel a lot more confident in your efforts for many reasons. For one, by keeping track of your contacts and the conversations you have with your pitching, you see proof of the work being done, which of course fuels you to move on and work harder at your media outreach. If you need any guidance on spreadsheets and how to use these programs, there are thousands of websites online that will walk you through any and all questions that you may have on using this type of software.

Many PR freelancers and larger agencies turn to major databases that usually charge monthly or yearly fees and are typically very expensive. If you are in a position financially and are willing to invest in your search for contacts, some of these resources include Cision, Muck Rack and Meltwater. These massive databases are usually updated more consistently than any individual or small business could do on their own. You can even create your list inside these programs to email directly to the media. I am going to assume that most of us reading this book are not in the position to purchase the above-mentioned resources, but it's good to know for the future.

As you grow your database of contacts and your career continues to develop, you may have more and more updates to provide to the media and you can simply service one by one every single time you want to communicate and update. Most of us are familiar with newsletters, open up your inbox and you'll probably have a couple sitting there as you read this book. I suggest using newsletters with caution, because in my opinion, you should have a certain reputation level built before you start blasting news to these contacts. As you would assume, the likelihood of someone reading your newsletter, especially as an artist, is much lower than directly reaching out to these people and writing a personal note.

Newsletters may be effective if you have something large in scale to announce such as a tour, a new album or even a line of merchandise that you are about to release. You must also be mindful that anyone that you add to your newsletter in the media should be tipped off or at least aware that they are on this list or you run the risk of getting unsubscribed. If that happens to you, don't take it personally. Think about those people that you added to the list that unsubscribed and understand why that may have happened. Some people just hate newsletters, as we are busier than ever in today's society and our time is so precious. On the flip side, it's kind of nice to have a well-organized update from someone that I appreciate, that's easy to read and has all the links that I need to find out more.

There are some newsletter programs available online for you to use that are free where the price point isn't tough to swallow. These newsletter programs allow you to import contacts from spreadsheets or by simply inputting each contact manually. You can even create different categories and tags within these newsletter programs so you can tip off a certain group of contacts specifically without having to email everyone every single time. Some programs that are popular include Mailchimp and Constant Contact. Again if you are looking for options simply jump on Google and search newsletter programs and try not to overthink it when making a decision. Lastly, I highly suggest only using newsletters when you have a solid fan base and a list of media contacts that appreciate what you're doing and know that you've been doing this for a while. I only open newsletters from sources that I signed up for or from at least those I may be interested in.

The point of this chapter is to keep your music life organized, that's really what matters. Musicians can be very impulsive and may spend a few hours one week reaching out to a bunch of people in the media and then a month later they forgot exactly what happened, who they reached out to and what those conversations were even about. I promise that if you take the basic steps of organizing and keeping notes on your efforts you will come off more professional and you'll have more clarity in your PR efforts.

16 - I'll see you online

I'm hoping that this brief book was informative and gave you a few "ah hah!" moments that inspire you to work smarter with your music-centric marketing. As a fellow musician and professional publicist, I encourage all my friends and those that seek my advice to brush up on their business knowledge in this ever-changing industry, and of course to crush it with their marketing. Marketing yourself is obviously an essential part of being at any level of working artist, and your efforts to build quality relationships within the media is something you'll thank yourself for later on.

While I usually advise artists to hire professionals for mostly everything outside of writing their music (well, people outsource that too), we have absolutely moved into an industry where it's easier than ever to self-produce, distribute, book shows and more. This book was designed to help artists understand how PR works, and if needed, how to handle it themselves if budgets don't allow for hiring a PR firm or consultant. There's too much great music out there to be heard, and it would be a shame for someone reading this to miss out on potentially well-deserved media exposure due to presumptions of how the PR machine works.

After completing this book, I encourage you to bookmark chapters that grabbed your interest. This guide will be here to walk you through steps you may have forgotten, and to help you spark ideas on what PR efforts may work best for you. Remember, always be patient and manage expectations with handling your own PR work. Also, be easy on yourself if you feel overwhelmed with the process. With anything, it takes time and repeated experience to get good at anything so always keep that in mind. And with that being said, there's no better time to start than now. Thanks for reading!

17 - But wait, there's more!

This is an alternate version of Chapter 9 on writing and structuring press releases, which I decided to include as it may help give you additional insight on crafting that perfect press release. This again includes a breakdown of each section along with a new example of a press release tailored to music. I hope this book and the information below is useful on your PR journey, and you can always find more examples of press releases on my website at BradleyPublicity.com.

Title - The headline of the press release is a one-sentence blip that will be the first thing anyone sees when looking at your media release for information. Think about it this way, when you open a blog, newspaper or see an article when scrolling on Facebook what is the first thing you notice? Yes, the headline! Without an attention-grabbing subject that is worthy of an editor's time or interest, you risk getting passed up before they even make the effort to read the details.

Keep the headline short and sweet, ideally being within 60-110 characters if possible. If you are hosting your release on PR Newswire or on your blog, you'll want to keep in mind that Google will be a major factor when it comes to SEO and finding the news organically. This headline gives the reader the one sentence update on what you have going on.

You can get a better idea on what headlines will work best for you by searching for other press releases online and even going on your favorite blogs to read article titles. Which ones grab your eye more than others? Put yourself in the shoes of the editor and readers when crafting this important part of the press release.

Summary - This 1 to 4 sentence section of the press release gives the reader a quick breakdown of what the news is about and reassures them that the story is indeed of interest to them. A headline can often be used simply as bait, and the summary can quickly break it down so the reader thinks "ah okay, that's what's going on here". For example, "Awesome indie band goes green for their album release event." Then the summary goes on to explain that they were part of a fundraising event where everyone in attendance including the band wore green and contributed $20 for a specific cause.

The summary can be creative or it can simply break down the details so busy editors can get to the point without having to read the entire release. A headline could read "Awesome indie band announces July West Coast trek with their friends in XYZ band as support". Then the summary quickly informs that there are 10 dates across Southern and Northern California, the band will be supporting the new album for the dates and that presale tickets will be available starting Friday.

Dateline - While press releases can vary in structure it's still important to have a dateline in the release. This is placed right below the summary and kicks off your press release. This informs the reader of the exact date the news went live and location of origin. So if you or your band is from New York, simply use that city to begin the dateline and follow-up with the month and day.

Body - The body of the press release can be multiple paragraphs and dishes out all the critical details about your exciting news. For the emerging artist reading this book, I advise to keep the body of your press release brief without sacrificing details that could be most helpful to the editor. The truth is that those in the media have less time than ever before, and at the time of writing this book, things have shifted dramatically in the world. Those that work in the media have had their world flipped upside down just like most other industries, and staying to the point and practicing brevity will be appreciated.

The press release body reiterates what you were implying in the headline, summary and beyond. This is your chance to talk about all the great things that are going on that are relevant to the headline of your press release. try your best not to go off-topic or speak of too many different things that could risk confusing the reader. Talking about a tour? Great! Stick with that information for 90% of your main body paragraphs. If you want to throw in additional details such as a new album, merchandise or a recent big media feature, make sure it fits within the context of your copy but don't place it at the top where your most critical information resets.

Every press release can be different, but I like to kick off the first paragraph with the most important details about your news in case the reader is short on time and is trying to gather as much information as possible. Any paragraphs after the first can include additional details about your news and relevant happenings that tie in with what you're talking about.

Think about it this way. If they don't read the rest of the paragraphs in the body will it make a difference if they decide to cover your news? If not, go back and consider trimming it down even more or at least feel confident that the additional details may not get read.

Links - It is important to include hyperlinks in your press release that point to websites and media that are relevant to the news. You can hyperlink words within the body of the press release and you can also have specific keyword links towards the bottom before your media contact information. You will see links structured in different ways in the different press releases you will see in your research. It is just important that these links are easy to find and that they actually work.

If the news is about a new music video, it may be smart to hyperlink the word music video or even music video for the song named in the body so if someone is curious to watch they can go to it immediately. Another great idea is to have a specific link for the music video somewhere else in the press release that is titled specifically. A good example would be "View new music video on Youtube" and link that specifically.

As I mentioned, I am not an SEO expert by trade. But I do know and I have been advised many times over the years that having great hyperlinks in your press release will help you with Google. Especially if you are hosting it on major press release aggregators and blogs that are searchable on Google and their competitors. At the least, you were making the lives of your reader just a little bit easier, and the icing on the cake is that your press release and news may be a bit more discoverable by keeping links in mind.

Keywords - On the SEO train again! Keeping select keywords in mind and including them throughout your press release may help the visibility of your news online. Ensuring that you are thinking about obvious words relevant to your specific news and genre of music is really all you need to do. While studying keywords in SEO never hurts, be sure to just include the keywords that identify best with you.

Boilerplate - A boilerplate is a brief description or snippet about the artist. While I've seen marathon long artist biographies, this is the place where the reader can quickly learn about you in 50-100 words. Specifically, if applicable this section includes any recent, relevant information to add to your credibility.

Contact and artist links - Including your contact information could be the difference between securing that media feature and losing it. Don't forget to include at least your email and phone number at the bottom. To keep it professional, put a title like "contact" and put your preferred contact methods below that so it's easy to read. Also include links to your website and social media territory so editors can learn more about you if interested.

Media assets - Include easy to find and read links so editors and writers can download critical assets such as press photos, album artwork, audio / video files and more. These files should be kept separately in any location like Google Docs, or a file-sharing program with an extended expiration date. Most people prefer something like Google Drive or Box, as it's easy to use and professional.

Embargoed release - If you need your news to be posted no sooner than X date, at the top of the release write something like "Please embargo for Monday, 5/5/20 at 8am PST" and underline and/or bold. Whatever it takes to make this critical note stand out so editors know not to post news before that day and time.

Press Release Example

The Social Distancers release their new single "Stay at home"

The 12 piece funk metal ska group celebrates 10 years of good times with a new single that will be included on their upcoming full-length album this spring.

(LOS ANGELES, CA) - April 15, 2020 - Southern California legends The Social Distancers (TSD) are at it again with the release of "Stay at home", their first single from the upcoming album 'When will this end?" set to drop this summer. Their unique blend of funk, metal and ska has earned the group one of SoCal's most diehard followings, and "Stay at home" delivers for the fans.

Recorded remotely by each band member at home, the group teamed up with acclaimed producer Joe Smith to produce and mix the single. While many artists have been creating live productions of their current catalog, TSD wanted to take things a step further with tracking and releasing their soon to be unveiled 4th full-length effort. Stepping up to the challenge, Smith worked with each band member to help track their instruments at home with Pro Tools and interface technology that would keep the quality to his standards.

The single stays true to TSD's unique sound, and has a darker/edgier tone with "Stay at home" as the band relates with the millions of other Americans stuck at home during lockdown. "While we're all bummed to be home for a while, we wanted to make the best of it and make an album that is fun but is relatable with what's going on" says Sarah Sounds, TSD's vocalist. "We hope our fans will dance in their living rooms to the track but also relate with the story I'm telling.".

"Stay at home" is available now on Apple Music, Spotify and most other online streaming platforms. Learn more about The Social Distancers at www.fakeartistwebsite.com

About The Social Distancers:

Los Angeles favorite The Social Distancers blend elements of funk, metal and ska better than anyone. Perhaps they may be the only of their kind, and this Los Angeles group prefers it that way. As the diverse group heads toward a decade of making music, the 12 piece outfit is currently working on the final touches for their 4th studio album ``When will this end?" to be released this summer. Don't miss out on what LA Weekly calls "The best party we've been to with the best-dressed band around, oh and it may get loud!"

Media Contact:

The Reader
Your Band Name
555.555.5555
Reader@YourBandName.com

For additional press release examples, visit BradleyPublicity.com or simply type "press release examples" into Google. Okay okay, now go get yourself some press! Thanks again for reading!